VOLLEYBALL

PLAYING WITH YOUR HEAD
AT ANY HEIGHT

Collin Henry
and Judy Corcoran

Wish Publishing
Terre Haute, Indiana
www.wishpublishing.com

LCCN: 2005936063

Editorial assistance provided by Cristina Gowrylow and Dorothy Chambers

Cover designed by Phil Velikan

Cover photography and interior photography provided by Yutaka Kawachi and Taka Studio

Printed in the United States of America
10 9 8 7 6 5 4 3 2 1

Published in the United States by
Wish Publishing
P.O. Box 10337
Terre Haute, Indiana 47801, USA
www.wishpublishing.com

Distributed in the United States by
Cardinal Publishers Group
Indianapolis, Indiana 46218

Table of Contents

Acknowledgements

Books are rarely written alone. We had lots of help with this one and we'd like to thank the following people: Yetunde Agbaje, Jennifer Berkley, Steve Bleuth, Ashley Carr, Belle Corcoran, Victoria Eisen Dine, The Ethical Culture Fieldston School, Nina Glinski, Sarah Hack, Agatha Henry, Molly Kawachi, Holly Kondras, Peter Thall, Wish Publishing and a special thanks to Yutaka Kawachi and Taka Studio.

 # Welcome to My Team

Whether you are taller than 6 feet or only a few inches more than 5 feet, welcome to my team. If you want to play competitive volleyball, it doesn't matter to me whether you can reach the top of the net with your elbow or the bottom of the net with your nose. If you are willing to work hard, set goals and make decisions, you can rule on the court.

Believe it, girl, there is room for you on the team. In fact, there's more than just room. You can be an important part of the team, even the captain – regardless of your height! That's right. It's not necessarily how tall you are, it's how smart you play the game that counts. And this book is going to tell you how to jump higher, hit harder, play smarter, lead your volleyball team to school and club championships, and pave the way to a position on a college team.

There is no getting around the fact that tall girls have an advantage in volleyball. In fact, if you are 6 feet tall, a coach might put you on a team regardless of your skill. The coach would tell you to stand in front of the net and stick your hands up when the ball comes over it. If you could master that, then you could learn other skills. If you are really tall *and* very athletic, then your volleyball career would have no bounds. But it doesn't really matter how tall you are because no amount of wishing will change your stature. So get comfortable with the size of your body. It may still be growing, and whatever size it ends up to be, it's yours for keeps. And the shape you keep it in is up to you.

So please, join my team. I can show you how to play the Jamaican way, which means you'll learn the different skills of volleyball one at a time. After you have mastered one skill, you can move on to the next. Playing volleyball is like speaking a foreign language. You can't just jump to Chapter 4 without mastering Chapters 1, 2 and 3. Volleyball should be taught in steps, and every step builds on the one before it. As you learn new skills, you will need to review the ones you already know, and you'll always be applying what you've just learned to what you learned last week. Then I'll tell you the proper way to execute each skill and finally, how to win matches. Hopefully you'll end up loving the game as well.

Have you figured out something here? There are no short cuts to becoming an outstanding volleyball player, but there is a method to it. It takes patience and time to learn to play volleyball the right way, so I want you to set small goals, ones that you can achieve in a few days. That way, every few days you will be able to say, "Look what I can do!" And when you get to that point, I want you to set a new goal.

But I also want you to set a big goal: to be the best player you can be. This book is for the serious volleyball player, for the girl who wants to win, improve and achieve her goals. You'll need to create room in your life to reach your goals, and every day you'll need to remind yourself of those goals. Winning tournaments and matches should be every team's goals, but they are not personal goals. They are barriers you need to cross to get to your bigger goals.

I am a serious coach, and when you join my team, I will tell you that you need to set goals and you will also need to make sacrifices. The loftier your goals, the bigger the sacrifices.

Sacrifice is a big part of any sport, but it's a huge part of volleyball. When the ball is about to touch the ground, there is no time to consider potential skinned knees or bruised elbows. There is only a split second for your body to extend beyond its size and pop the unreachable ball back up into play. That second, when only the extra effort of a desperate lunge can save a play, puts the impossible within your reach.

Extra effort can't be taught. It comes from the heart, springing from your desire to excel, to use all of your abilities and knowledge to be the best. Challenging the impossible takes maximum effort, but that's what separates the average players from the great ones. It also makes for some really outstanding volleyball.

Outstanding players practice a lot. If you practice volleyball for three hours a day for the next three years, you will reach a certain level as a player. If you practice more than that, if you do 150 crunches when the coach asks for 100, or 40 push-ups when the coach asks for 20, you will reach an even higher level as a player. There is a point where you have to make a decision as to whether you want to be an outstanding volleyball player or an average one.

When I was 15 years old, I was asked to join the team at the Jamaican national volleyball training camp. I was already a good runner and jumper in track and field, and I was tall at 6 feet 6 inches. Regardless, I went to their camp for eight weeks. Each day we'd get up at 6 a.m. to run five miles, stretch and do regular conditioning, and we'd do 1,000 sets and 1,000 digs right before official practice started. If the ball hit the ground, we had to start over. And we all wanted to finish this task before the Jamaican sun reached its full strength.

The coach, Mr. Cameron, always had a number in his head of how many sets or digs he'd let us do, and he'd usually stop us after 5,000. But when I realized that I couldn't do 1,000 straight, I'd keep doing them. I learned early on that if you have an opponent who is at the same level, you need to outdo him or her. If she trains for 10 hours a week, you need to train for 15. After camp that summer, I went straight to the Jamaican national men's team as the team's youngest player.

You Need a Motto

To succeed at volleyball, you need to develop a motto, and I suggest that you write it down somewhere so you can refer to it. In it you need to make a promise to yourself. It can be whatever you want it to be. "I'm going to give 110% today." "I'm going to dig 30 balls today." "I'm going to work really hard today." The motto I used was very personal to me. "I'm using sports to get away," was my motto. I was born in a very poor area of Jamaica and my family had no money. Volleyball offered me a way out, a ticket to a new life.

Let your motto inspire you to achieve more, to jump higher and dig harder. Take it home with you and rather than sit in front of the television, use your motto to review your practice or to do some squats. If you really need to sit in front of the TV, watch a videotape of a college match. There are some available from the NCAA or USA Volleyball, and you can usually find college games on a sports channel on weekends from September to December.

Some Basics

In addition to developing a motto and setting small goals, here are some more basics to follow as a member of my team. *Never play a game without the proper shoes and kneepads.* I don't like to see anyone get hurt, so this is my first rule. I like to wear ankle guards when playing games as well, but that is up to you. There is nothing worse than warming up for a big game, then coming down on the edge of your sneaker and spraining your ankle. It's pretty bad when it happens during a game, but it's even worse when it happens just *before* a big game. At first it really hurts, and since no one knows how severe it is, you'll have to sit out the big game with a sack of ice on your ankle. It may be better the next day, but there may not be a game the next day, as this was the BIG game. Ankle guards will protect you, as will knee pads, so wear them.

Another basic is to get a volleyball for your home. It doesn't matter whether you live in a big house or small apartment, because all I want you to do is carry that ball around with you. I want it to be the last thing you put down before you go to bed and the first thing you pick up in the morning. I want your hands to learn the size and weight of it. I want you to become comfortable with it, balancing it on your arms and in your hands and touching it with your fingers.

The First Day

On the first day of practice, I start by having everyone introduce herself and share the reason she is choosing volleyball over another sport. It is especially important for shorter girls to explain the reasons they want to succeed in what is perceived as a tall girl's sport. Perhaps you are coming from gymnastics and have extraordinary upper body strength. Maybe your older sister and family play the game. Maybe you just really like volleyball. Maybe you just really dislike soccer.

After that, I ask the girls to set a big goal for the season and small goals for the weeks ahead. As a team, the big goal might be to win the state championship, and the small goal might be to win the next match. As an individual, a big goal might be to get athletic scholarship money for college, and a small goal might be to make all the serves go over the net in the next game. Small goals work better than large goals because you won't get discouraged with small goals. It's like losing weight, something most girls know about. Sure, you want to lose 10 pounds by next week, but setting the goal of losing two pounds a week for five weeks is an achievable goal, whereas 10 pounds in one week isn't.

At the first practice I tell you what we can expect from each other and warn you about the sacrifices you will be making as a team and as individuals. I want you to compete as a competitor, not just a player, so I expect you to give 110% every time you practice and to make volleyball an after-school priority.

Achieving in school is your first priority, and if you can't do your school work, you can't be on my team. Many girls find that practicing and playing volleyball enables them to study more efficiently. One girl told me that by 3:00, she was burnt out on school, and that practicing volleyball gave her a needed break from the academic pressure. By the time volleyball was over, she was ready to study again.

There will be times when you have a big test and may need to forego practice, but that shouldn't happen every week and for every subject. Successful players know they need to do their school work before it is due, and they can't wait till the last minute to write a paper. If you have a big test coming, bring a study sheet to practice with you. When you are resting your body during practice, review your study sheet. If someone on the team is in the same class, ask her to be your partner that day at practice and repeat the facts you need to study or know while you are warming up or working out. Also, if you can, get your SAT tests out of the way as early as possible.

The Rules

If you are on my team, you will also need to abide by some rules. Most coaches probably have their own rules, and I'm telling you mine just so you can see what I expect of my team. They are:

1. *Call me if you will be late or missing practice.* Personal emergencies, family occasions, injuries, holidays and school obligations are the acceptable reasons for lateness and absence from practice, but be prepared to bring a note from your parents or guardian explaining this.

2. *If you are the leader of an organization, you need to ask them to appoint another leader until the end of the season.* You may want to be editor of the school newspaper and play volleyball, but you may have to make a choice here. Both will demand your time, and it's better to choose before the season starts rather than get caught up in a conflict later on.

3. *Explain your commitment to volleyball to your friends before there is a problem.* Volleyball may interfere with some of your friendships because you won't have time to hang around with all of your friends. You'll need to talk to

14

them and explain your goals, and make a specific time to be with them or meet up with them. Most importantly, you need to make sure they understand this. If they want you to hang out when you have practice, ask your coach for an open practice so that your friends can come and watch you play.

4. *Prepare a timetable that balances practice, studying and your other obligations.* Write on it any assignments or upcoming special circumstances that you know about. If you have a paper due in three weeks, start now and map out your plan for doing your research and for your writing. I may ask you to show this timetable to me throughout the course of the season.

5. *Everyone must always be at practice 15 minutes before starting time and 45 minutes before the ref whistles for the captains. You should be on the court 45 minutes before the ref blows the whistle that signals the captains to begin official warm-ups.* I also tell my team that when it comes to game day, I don't pick who plays — you do. You do by showing everyone how hard you want to play, how much you want to win, and how far you're willing to go. You show me this in practice before the game, so get there early and prepare for it.

6. *Expect practice to be as demanding as a game.* The environment in which you practice or work out should always be a game-like environment and in a gym. The intensity must be the same as the game so I will set that pace at practice. If the practice sessions are too easy, your brain will not learn to perform in a stressful environment.

Coaching Boundaries

As a coach, my girls can expect me to be there for them all the time, not only as a coach but as a teacher, a mentor, an example of the sport, and most of all, as a friend in a respectable way. But I do have boundaries, which I discuss in detail in Chapter 11.

As your coach, I should know when you are not feeling well, when you are distracted and when you are injured, and you should talk to me about these things at practice. If you are having problems or troubles that are affecting your game, you should tell me at practice. If you are having problems at home, at school or with your friends, and just want to talk to me, you can do that before or after practice.

Let me just say a word about coaches here. Many coaches are great, but unfortunately some could be better. I'll talk more about coaching in Chapter 11, but for now let's just agree that there is no one right way for every girl to perform a certain skill. Girls have different body types, strengths and physical abilities. A coach should find ways to make them better players rather than try to change their style of playing. If a coach tells you to toss the ball higher but that just doesn't work for you, you'll need to talk to him or her and explain that. Most coaches will appreciate your effort and honesty.

Conditioning

While you are learning skills, I will also give you exercises to do. But don't expect me to say, "Okay, do 20 push-ups," because that will only help build your upper-body strength. I know you are all able to multitask because I know you can send Instant Messages to seven people at once on the computer or that you can study with the television on, so when I assign a strengthening exercise, it will work on two areas at once. And this doesn't make it twice as hard, just twice as good. For instance, instead of doing push-ups, I may want you to place the volleyball on the floor, put your palms around the ball and then do the push-ups. You have hundreds of muscles in your hands and fingers that will be used in volleyball, and you will need to strengthen them as well. Pushing up on a volleyball will strengthen your fingers and hands while it works your arm and shoulder muscles in the exact motion needed for volleyball.

The reason for this multitasking is that doing more than one thing at once is what volleyball is all about. You step and hit at the same time, just as you talk and listen at the same time. You jump and block at the same time. You serve and cover at the same time. By teaching you to do two things at once in a physically stressful environment, I'm training your mind to play volleyball and to make the right decision while taking a physical action. And I'm also training your body to function regardless of your mind's stress. So remember that every exercise I assign will be related to a skill of the game, and every drill will be specific to a skill or combination of skills.

One more word about conditioning. Before you start playing in a game or at practice, you should always warm up your muscles and joints. When you finish, you must stretch out those muscles in order to avoid lots of injuries. There is more about conditioning in Chapters 2 and 4.

Playing Other Sports

Speaking of doing two things at once, if you play volleyball on a club or travel team in the winter and spring and want to play another sport at school, such as basketball or track, you'll need to carefully weigh the risks of injury from over-training. Many volleyball players are asked to play basketball during its season, and they end up practicing two hours a day, then going to club volleyball for another two hours in the evening. This can lead to fatigue which often leads to injuries such as stress fractures, sprains, torn and ruptured ligaments, any of which can be career threatening or ending.

Before joining another team, talk to your parents and coach about the effects of the additional training and whether your body can handle it. Things to consider are past injuries, present sore spots, the nature of the other sport and the competitive level of the other team. Swimming may be a better complement to volleyball than basketball, especially if the basketball team is expected to win a championship.

At the same time, you don't want to be at a complete rest at the end of your season, because that isn't good for your body either. You need to take an active rest, with sports like swimming, biking, yoga, weight lifting and other cardiovascular exercises and stretching.

Training with Weights

Some people think that high school girls shouldn't lift weights. I believe you should lift light weights but only enough to make it challenging. Using 2- and 3-pound weights should be enough for curls and shoulder presses. Doing these exercises with a light weight is a lot less pressure on the muscles and bones than hitting a volleyball. If you work and train those muscles, you will hit and serve a volleyball more easily and avoid injuries as well.

Before you train with weights, however, you should learn how to lift them properly in order to train your muscles to protect your joints. I will describe proper weight-lifting techniques in later chapters. To begin, you should know never to lift weights without supervision, because you could develop bad habits or injure yourself. If your coach isn't well versed in lifting weights, try to find a trainer who is certified by the American Council on Exercise (ACE), the National Council on Strength and Fitness (NCSF), or is affiliated with a gym in your area. See whether you can work with a trainer at a gym or in your home once every few weeks, so that he or she can check to see that you're working in the proper positions and not lifting too much weight. It is better to use light weights and do more repetitions than use heavier weights with fewer repetitions. If you don't have a trainer to work with, ask your parents to help you look at some of the many videotapes on weight lifting that are available to young women. Lifting light weights builds muscle, not mass, meaning your muscles won't get bigger with light weights, only stronger.

I also believe in resistance training and will suggest exercises with rubber bands or resistance tubes and medicine balls. Rubber bands can be purchased at most athletic equipment stores or on the Internet. Setters may want to get a setter's ball which is heavier than a regular volleyball and is used in training.

Finding the Balance

In addition to patience and strength, you need balance to play volleyball. Volleyball is filled with stretching and reaching, hitting on the run, and digging the ball off the ground. I will suggest some exercises and drills to increase your balance.

Along with physical balance, a successful volleyball player also needs to balance her life. You need to balance your school work with your practice schedule. You need to balance what you eat before and after a game with what you regularly eat. You need to balance your friends with your teammates. You need to balance your coach with your parents. And you need to balance your mind with your body, and learn to get over mistakes quickly, especially when you're in the middle of a game.

If you want to play volleyball in college, you can — at any height. You just have to find the right team for your skills. If you want to play for Stanford or USC, you will probably need to be tall, and you will most likely have to make thousands of sacrifices throughout your high school career. But being a shorter volleyball player doesn't automatically put you out of Division I schools. On last year's roster, Penn State had a libero (L) who was 5 foot 6 inches tall, two back row players who were each 5 foot 4 inches tall and a defensive specialist (DS) who was 5 foot tall. Ohio State has a libero who was 5 foot 3 inches tall. The DS/L at University of Wisconsin was 5 foot 4 inches tall. University of Illinois had a 5 foot 5 inches tall DS. The setter for Harvard a few years ago was 5 foot 3 inches tall. Yale had a 5 foot 5 inches tall DS. The list goes on.

Pick a school and go to its website, click on athletics, women's volleyball and roster. From the UConn Huskies who have a DS/L who is 5 foot 3 inches tall to the Connecticut College Camels who have an outside hitter who is 5 foot 6 inches tall, you will find a college team that is right for you. In all, there are 411 Division III schools with women's volleyball teams, 265 Division II schools, and 313

Division I. In addition, most Division I schools have Club teams which often have varsity-level payers and are equally competitive.

So whether you have more than four years until college or less than one, you should make a time table and set your small and large goals. And now that you're on my team, you'll want to read on, but remember that this is not a miracle book. If you're having trouble finding your own balance and deciding what is really important to you, you'll need to do some homework. You'll need to assess your priorities and abilities and decide what you want for yourself.

Lots of coaches can lead a team to victory, but very few coaches can teach skills. I can tell you how to serve, hit, set and pass the right way. I can show you how you can rule on the court, and how to play with your head at any height. I can give you tools, guidance and suggestions on how to make volleyball fit into your life, but only you can do the work necessary to become an outstanding volleyball player.

 The Overhead Pass or Set: Where it All Starts

The overhead pass or set is generally reserved for the setter. But everyone should learn it because there are many instances when you will need it, such as when your setter is in the back row, passing or digging the ball, or when she can't get to the ball and calls for help. You may want to use an overhead set to pass a float serve that doesn't have much movement to it, a free ball or a very slow jump or top spin serve.

If you're already playing on a volleyball team, you probably know how to set a ball or use the overhead pass, but it's always good to review the proper technique. That way, your feet, hips, body weight, arms, hands, fingers, head and eyes are all working for you, going in the right direction and giving you the max for your effort. Practicing the fundamentals in volleyball is like a golfer practicing her swing or a batter checking his stance. When your position and motion are textbook correct, every play you make will turn out better.

If you feel really comfortable with the technique that follows and tend to get it quickly, you have the makings of a setter. If you are a shorter girl with very good hands, body and ball control, your future as a setter is almost certain.

The Perfect Motion for an Overhead Pass

Here is a 10-step method to develop the perfect motion for an overhead pass. Before you start any kind of physical exercise or training, however, you need to warm up. Start out by tossing a volleyball gently in the air and catching it. Then dribble it on the floor and bounce it off a wall, first with one arm, then with the other, and then with both.

1. Find a bench or a chair without arms and sit on it. Spread your fingers as wide as they can go and touch the top of each finger on your left hand to each finger on your right hand. Your arms are perpendicular to the floor, with your elbows bent and slightly forward from your shoulders. Look through your thumbs and index fingers at your pinkies. Look closely at the front and side views below.

 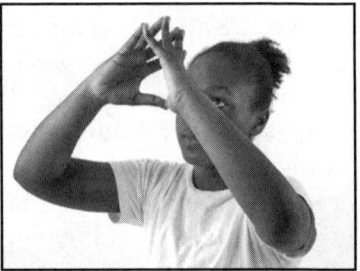

2. Now raise your arms from your shoulders and bend your head back so that your hands are three to four inches above your forehead and you're still looking at the space between your thumbs and index fingers. Notice the front and side views in the photos. Then open the space between your fingers to about one or two inches, keeping your hands in the shape of the volleyball.

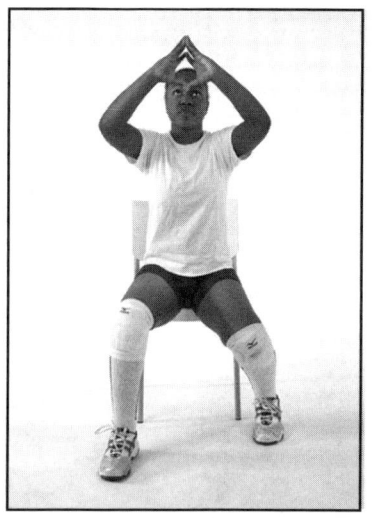 

3. Next, position your right leg so that it is slightly for-
    ward from the chair and move your left leg to the side
    of the chair and back slightly. Balance your left foot on
    your toes. Now stand up and sit down, in that posi-
    tion, 10 times. End by sitting down.

4. Lift your arms over your head with your fingers in that
    same position, as if holding a volleyball, with your

thumbs one to two inches apart. Then stand up and extend your arms by pushing through with your thumbs, pushing them toward your target. Do this a few times.

5. Then, sit, stand, extend your arms, push with your thumbs, and follow through by stepping forward with your back leg.

6. Next, add the ball to your hands. Stand with the ball and extend your arms with it. Grip the ball so that your index fingers and thumbs are about one-and-a-half inches apart. Get a feel for the arm motion with the ball in your hands. Do this motion about 10 times. If you have small hands, make sure your index fingers and thumbs are wide enough so that the ball sits firmly on your fingers. If your neck starts to hurt from looking up at the ball, stop for a few minutes and stretch it out by gently rotating your head in full circles, and then side to side and back to front, holding each position for about five seconds. As you continue these skills, your neck muscles will become stronger.

7. In that same sitting position on the chair or bench, with your arms fully extended, bounce the ball off the floor with a flick of your wrists and catch it near your forehead. Then, from the sitting position, lift your entire body and the ball up toward the ceiling. Repeat several times.

8. Then put it all together – sit, push the ball to the floor, catch it near your forehead, stand with the ball and extend your arms over your head. Don't release the ball in this exercise. Sit again, and repeat this exercise a few times.

 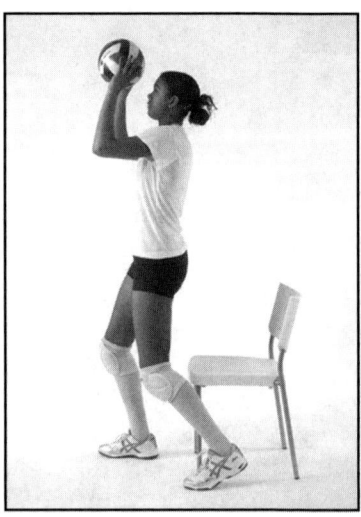

Add the ball to the sit, stand and extend positions.

9. From a standing position, with your right leg in front, body leaning forward, left leg out to the side and three to four feet behind the right foot, set the ball onto the floor as you did while you were sitting, and catch it. Then bring your body up from that crouched position, with the ball three inches above your forehead. Check your hands and shoulders. Make sure your fingers are spread wide, and your hands make contact with the ball at the same place each time, with the same distance between your thumbs and index fingers. Your elbows should bend at the same angle.

Set the ball to the floor, catch it and bring it up to your forehead.

10. Take the same standing position but move away from the bench and face a wall. Stand one foot from the wall, bounce the ball off the wall and catch it three inches from your forehead. Then release it with a full push of the arms and thumbs. How far the ball goes depends on how fast you push. Long, high sets take a fast arm motion with extended wrists. Then repeat the exercise, standing two feet and then three feet from the wall. When you feel comfortable, catch and push the ball from even farther away.

Notice the extension of the arms and how the thumbs follow through.

You'll eventually find your own comfort zone. But try to remember the correct motion as you warm up and practice. You might want to go back to the bench position mentioned in Step 8 and review that before each practice. At this point, you don't have to catch the ball anymore; you can set the ball to the floor and then off the wall.

When you're practicing with a partner, ask her to toss the ball to you so you can catch it in the setting position. Hold on to the ball and ask her to check that your position is correct. Then toss the ball to her and check her position. Start at three feet apart and move farther away from each other. Then repeat this with one person setting and the other person tossing the ball. Check your positions as you go.

Returning Serve with Overhead Pass

When making contact with a served ball, think overhead pass, not set. The difference is your target. In an overhead pass, your target is the setter. In a set, your target is the attacker.

The speed of the oncoming ball dictates how much push you will need to get the ball to your target. It's best to return a serve with an overhead pass when the ball is served high and drops slowly. Trying an overhead pass on a ball with top spin or on a jump serve could jam or injure your fingers because of the ball's oncoming power and speed. Use your overhead pass on a high float serve that has little or no movement to it and on free ball or when you have plenty of time to get under the ball and into the ready position.

The Ready Position

The ready position for the overhead pass (as well as for those receiving in the back court) is the balanced base. Your feet are a little wider than your shoulders and your knees are slightly bent. You want to keep a light movement in the feet, not be flat footed, with your body weight forward. If your toes are pointed out rather than parallel, it's easier to move in any direction. Your shoulders should be relaxed and your arms above your waist and bent at the elbow. Your hands are up, a few inches from your forehead, with your fingers extended in the shape of a volleyball. Your thumbs and index fingers form a triangle, with about one to two inches of space between them. You shouldn't see your palms, as they are not parallel nor facing forward, but in a "U" shape. Your thumbs should be pointing back toward your eyes or nose, or even each other, and never pointing forward.

If you are passing from the right side of the court, keep your right leg in front. That way, your body is facing into

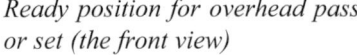

Ready position for overhead pass or set (the front view)   *Ready position for overhead pass or set (the side view)*

the court. If you are passing from the left, keep your left leg in front and again, your body will be facing your target. If you are passing from the middle, it doesn't matter which leg is in front, as long as you keep one leg in front for balance and better body control. See the photos on passing in Chapter 5.

Always make an overhead pass from a wide base and with your leading leg facing the target.

Contact with the Ball

Start your hand and arm motion when the ball is about one to two inches away from your hands. You don't want to catch the ball and push it away. You want to meet the ball with your push. That's the reason your hands need to be up and ready before the ball gets to you. You meet and reverse the ball's momentum with a spring-like action in your wrists and fingers. You must have some strength in your hands and fingers before trying to set a served ball, and the touch on the ball should be light but firm. If not, the ball will go through your fingers.

You should extend your arms, but the amount of extension depends on the speed at which the ball is coming over the net. If the ball is slow, then you will need to push more. A faster ball needs a quick release from the wrist and firmer fingers with little arm movement.

Set with soft hands and a strong spring-like action.

When you contact the ball, cradle it primarily with the first part or knuckle of your thumbs and your index and middle fingers, all the way to the second knuckles, and never in the palm of your hands. Your ring finger and pinkie should touch the ball, even though they rarely do. When they do, you will have better control on the ball, especially if your hands are very small.

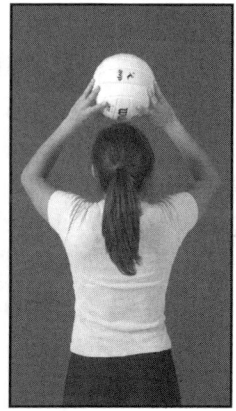

Correct position of fingers on the ball for overhead pass or set (the front, side and back views)

To properly execute an overhead pass or set, your body must be squarely under the ball. If your hands are in the correct position, and you were told to open them just as the ball gets there, the ball would hit you on your forehead.

Be careful not to catch the ball with your arms fully extended. If you do, you won't have the space for the pushing motion, which is what gets the ball back to the target. You will also most likely be called for holding the ball, because now you have to bring it down in order to push it out.

Incorrect position for contact with the ball: Hands are too high over the head and leave no space to push the ball. Also, in this position, the ball might go through your fingers or you may be called for holding the ball.

Push with Your Thumbs

Extend your arms and finish the set with your thumbs. Your thumbs and index fingers are the last two fingers off the ball. These fingers are the primary weapons in the set and overhead pass. The other fingers are used for balance and stability of the ball.

> **In an overhead pass, always end by pointing your thumbs toward your target.**

Weight Shift

Follow through by stepping forward with your back leg. Right before you push the ball with your arms, shift your weight in the direction of the target. Shifting weight from your back leg to your front leg gives you more power in your arms and can improve your accuracy. As you shift your body weight, the momentum should take the leg from the back to the front. This step happens *after* you release the ball, not *as* you release the ball.

Your first step should always be in the direction of the ball. Many players lean back to set the overhead or reach to their left or right with only their hands. The only correct position is behind the ball, so you can go forward, to the ball, to reach it.

Normally your right leg is in front but it doesn't really matter, unless you are setting the ball near the net from either side of the court. If you are setting from the net, then you always want your right foot forward so that you rotate away from and not toward the net. Having one leg in front gives you better range and control of both the ball and your body. The weight shift from back to front and the follow through of the leg in back gives you the ability to move more freely to hit or cover the hitter.

Proper setting positions: Ready position and contact (the front and side views)

33

The Secret Is in Your Feet

The secret to a successful overhead pass is getting your feet into position first. If your feet are in the right place, your body and arms will be there too. If your toes are pointed out, not parallel, it is easier to move in any direction. When you step, always step with your left leg toward the ball and your right leg toward your target. After moving from point A to point B, the finish motion with the feet is a slight hop, which will enable the body to establish a quicker setting base.

Left leg ball/Right leg target

Avoid the Two-Handed Touch

A two-handed touch is called when you contact the ball with one hand before the other. If your hands are not evenly spaced when you contact the ball, it may look like a two-handed touch, so make sure that your hands, fingers and body are all in the same line with the ball.

Also, keep your hands in the correct position as you raise them to your forehead. Make sure both hands are over your forehead and ready to set the ball before the ball gets too close to your forehead. This will help prevent the double hit. If your hands come apart on contact with the ball, then you have them spread too far apart or your fingers aren't strong enough (see Wall Push-Ups on Finger Tips to strengthen your fingers).

If one hand gets there before the ball and the other one gets there as the ball reaches your forehead, you will have an uneven contact, which will send the ball off to the side. This generates more force, and the referee will call you for a double contact or hit.

Small Hands

If you have small hands, you should separate your thumbs two to three inches and contact the ball more to the side than underneath. You may also learn to release the ball more quickly, as some refs may call you for holding the ball when you're actually just placing your hands in a more comfortable position for their size. Make sure your fingers are spread out as well.

Notice the hand placement on the ball for small hands (top) and large hands (bottom) for an overhead pass and set. With smaller hands, the fingers are more spaced out, the hands are wider apart, and the index fingers and thumbs are much farther away from each other. Compare them to the larger hands in the bottom photo.

Avoiding Lifts

A lift is called when you hold on to the ball for too long and then try to set it or pass it overhead. You can avoid lifts by making contact with the ball above your forehead. If you start your overhead pass or set at chest level, or if your hands are so high that you have to bring the ball down to push it back up, you'll probably hear a whistle blow.

Conditioning for Overhead Pass

Any exercise that increases your upper body strength will help you build your shoulders and triceps. This in turn will make it easier for you to play harder and longer. But before you work out, always make sure you warm up and cool down properly. See Chapter 4 for specifics on warming up and stretching out your shoulders, and then try these exercises.

One-Hand and Two-Hand Push-Ups on a Volleyball

Place a volleyball on the floor. Lie down next to it in a push-up position, and place the volleyball under your right hand. Start with bent-knee push-ups if you need to and push up from there. Then switch the volleyball to your left hand. This exercise builds your hand and finger muscles along with your shoulder, triceps and back muscles. If you are strong enough, go to a full or regular push-up on the ball. Then try pushing up with both hands on the ball, starting again with bent knees and progressing to a regular push-up.

Wall Push-Ups on Finger Tips

Face a wall and position your feet three feet way. Place your finger tips on the wall and pushup from there. Again, you will build shoulder, triceps and back muscles along with strengthening your fingers. Next hold the ball on the wall and push up off the ball.

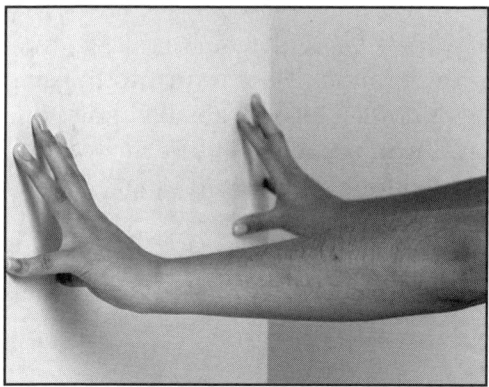

Wall push-ups on finger tips help strengthen the fingers, especially for setters.

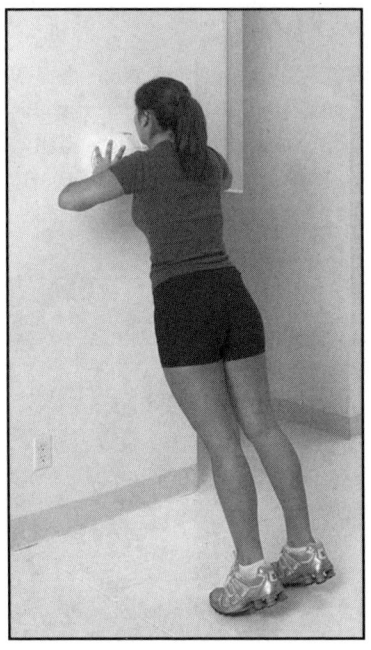 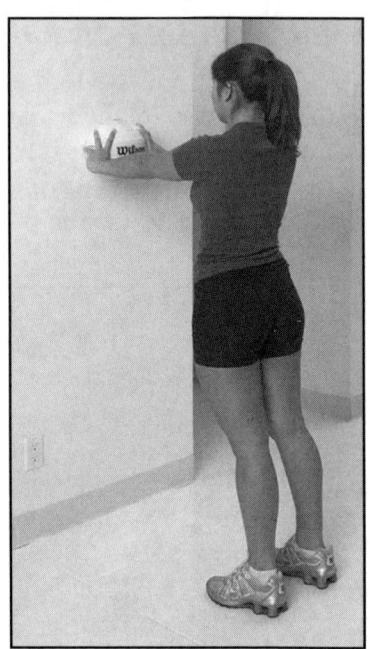

Wall push-ups on the volleyball

Walking/Tossing Lunges

Take a step forward with your right leg and bend your left knee to the ground. Then return to the standing position and walk your left leg in front, bending your right knee to the ground. Add a volleyball to your walking lunges by tossing and catching it while you lunge.

Skips

Skip across the court while you are setting and catching the ball.

Bed Sets

Lie flat on your bed and set the ball above your forehead. Then add a heavier medicine or setter's ball, but don't miss!

Shoulder Press

Standard shoulder presses, where your arms extend upward from your shoulders past your ears, with 2- to 3-pound weights or resistance bands (pictured below), will increase your strength.

Pull-Ups

From a sturdy bar a few inches above your tallest reach, grab hold and raise your body up and down 10 times.

Resistance Bands

If you have access to resistance bands, use them for shoulder presses and triceps push-ups. In a shoulder press, the resistance comes from raising and extending your upper arm from your shoulder. In a triceps push-ups, the resistance comes from moving your forearm or triceps away from your upper arm, starting with your elbows bent.

To do the **shoulder press**, sit on a bench and lock the resistance band under it. Bring your hands with the bands up to your shoulders. The press starts from the ears, pushes up over the head, and releases back down to the ears. Do three sets of 15.

Shoulder press with resistance bands – start and finish

From the same seated position, do the **triceps push-up**. Drop your hands behind your head and point your elbows to the ceiling. Now extend your hands from your elbows to the ceiling. Do three sets of 15.

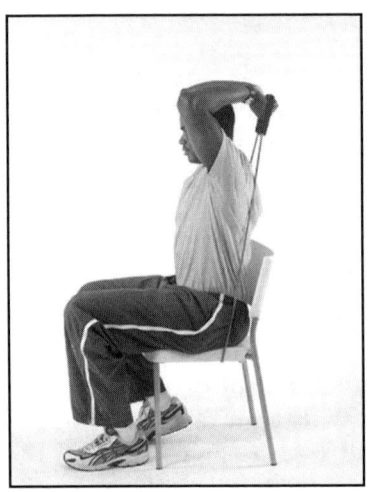 

Triceps push-up with resistance bands – start and finish

Hands and Fingers

Try these exercises to strengthen and stretch your hands and fingers:

1. *Finger Stretch.* Hold your hands out in front of you, palms facing down. On each hand, draw your fingers together so they are all touching, including your thumb. Then spread your fingers apart and stretch them as far as they can go. Do this 10 times. Next do this with your wrists flexed upward and then downward.

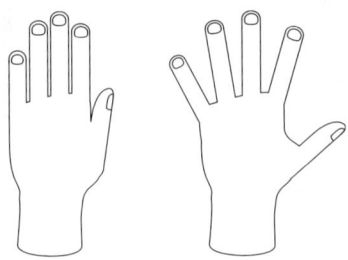

2. *Finger Push-Ups.* Hold your hands in a prayer position, with palms touching and fingers spread out. Press your fingers out so that your palms separate and your thumbs and pinkies are parallel to the ground. Then bring your fingers back together with your finger tips still touching, so that they all touch each other. Do this 15 times.

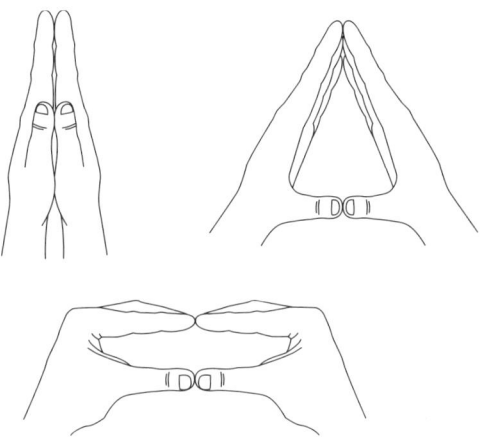

3. *Wrist Push.* Put your hands in the prayer position with your elbow out and forearms parallel to the ground. Feel the stretch in your wrists as your hold for 15 seconds. Then reverse the action with the backs of your hands together and your fingers pointing down.

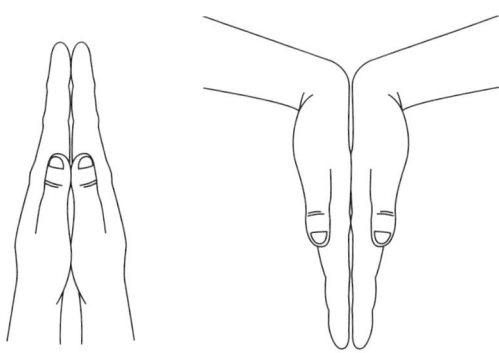

4. *Wrist Bend.* With your arms extended in front of you, bend your wrists down with fingers pointing to the floor and hold for five seconds. Do this five times. Then reverse the direction and bend your wrists up, holding and releasing.

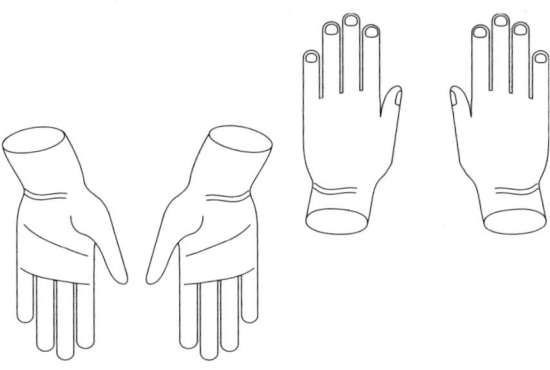

5. *Wrist Twist.* With your arms extended in front of you, about shoulder width apart, hold a towel in both hands and pull apart. Twist one wrist forward and one backward, and then twist the other direction. Do this five times.

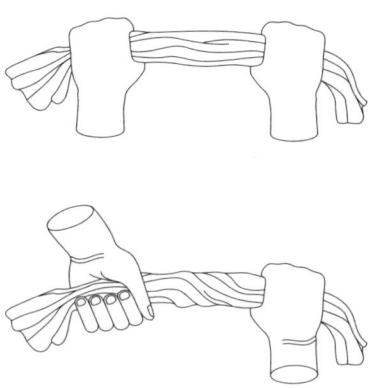

The Setter: The Soul of the Team

Like the quarterback in football, the setter runs the offense in volleyball. She "sets" up the attack, deciding which girl on her team is in the best position to make the kill. She is often the soul of the team, keeping everyone together and dictating the tempo of the game.

As the leader on the court, the setter has to be smart, quick and vocal. She is a gentle giant who gets along with everyone on the team, but her attitude and rhythm are different from the other members. She is aggressive but calm, firm but flexible. She is someone who can scream at you without hurting your feelings; someone who can handle a stressful situation while keeping her calm.

Not only does the setter need the right personality, she needs a broader knowledge of the game than the other players. While a defensive specialist or libero needs to think about passing the ball, and the hitter needs to think about attacking the ball, the setter needs to run the entire offense inside her head. Before the ball is served, she chooses her strongest offensive play depending on how her hitters match up with the opponent's blockers. As soon as the ball is served to her team, she springs into action, often changing her offense as the ball takes an unexpected turn. It's not until the ball is received and passed that she puts into action the actual offensive play or if needed, her emergency backup play. While she plans her moves in the pre-serve huddle and starts her job after the ball is in play, she depends on the passers in the back row to do their job effectively so that she can do hers.

A setter doesn't have to be tall, but she must be quick. When the ball is passed from the back row, she is there, waiting to send the perfect overhead set to one of her hitters. But if the pass goes badly, she must get to the ball quickly and put it in a good spot where her attackers will get a chance for a kill or maybe just keep the ball in play.

The setter calls the plays. Whether she calls out names or numbers, or holds up fingers, she tells the others what she wants to happen. A setter at the high school level should know the best play for a particular rotation, but the coach plays an important part here. At times, the coach will have a better perspective on what's happening in both ends of the court and should tell the setter the best play, then let her communicate with the rest of the team.

Most of all, the setter needs exceptional awareness of the total court. She should know the location of her hitters and the opponent's blockers. Obviously, her overhead passes or sets must be consistent and her ball control must be solid. She must have a large variety of sets at her fingertips, and she should know the individual styles or preferences of her hitters. If her best hitter is in the middle and likes her sets two-and-a-half feet rather than one foot above the net, the setter should know. And the setter should know whether her hitter is having a good day or a bad day, and if it's a bad day, whether that's because of something that happened before or during the game.

Setting the Ball

Before the setter makes contact with the ball, she first needs to step toward it with her left foot to help square her body with the net, and then step toward her target with her right foot. Her knees are bent and her body leans slightly forward. As the ball comes toward her, the contact is close to her forehead, and she pushes it away, just like an overhead pass. After the ball is pushed into motion and her arms are fully extended, her left leg follows through from the back in a forward motion, taking her into the coverage position. A good setter always covers the attacker after she makes the set. That's why it is so important to have your feet pointed in the right direction and moving before you make the set, even with a perfect pass.

Ready position and first step for the setter where the body squares up during the set with the right leg in front

The Jump Set

The position for the jump set is essentially the same as with a regular set, except that you jump as high as you can as you set the ball. With a jump set, the left/right footwork is used to square your body before you take off so that you don't have that extra rotation coming from your waist after you jump. The left/right approach allows you to jump into the ball, which is what you want. You should always try to go for your maximum jump to give yourself some more time to make the set. The way to get your maximum jump is to use the spike approach, which in setting usually starts with the left foot as well. You will get a better understanding of the jump set approach in Chapter 6, the chapter on hitting.

A jump set helps to make a much quicker set to the middle, and when you are in the front court, the blockers won't know whether you are going to tip or set the ball. In a jump set, use a back swing of the arms into the jump and show your setting hands early to the ball after the jump. Push with full extension of the arms and hold that extension until your feet hit the floor.

Taking It to the Court

Here is the layout of the court. The setter's primary setting position is on the front and right side of the court, about one foot from the net, between positions 2 and 3. Every other movement comes after she gets to that spot. Even though she will not get all the passes at that spot, her job is to get there before the ball is passed and then go wherever the ball takes her. In all six rotations,

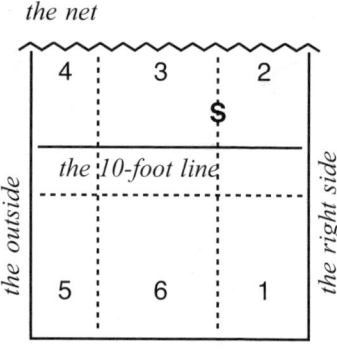

the net

the setter in the front court

that spot is the easiest position to start her offense, and it gives her an overall view of the entire court (see diagram of fifth rotation on page 49).

While the setter's primary defensive position on the front court is on the right side of the net, when she is in the back court, she is on the right side behind the 10-foot line.

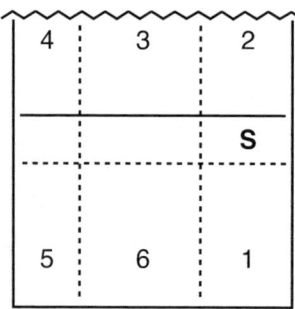

The setter in the back court

The Starting or First Rotation

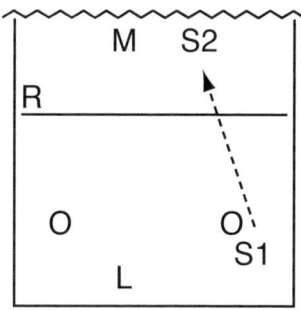

Setting after you serve is called first rotation or position 1. (See diagram. Note that in each diagram S1 indicates where the setter starts and S2 shows where she goes. O stands for the passers or outside hitters. L is libero, R is the right side or opposite hitter and M is the middle hitter.) In this rotation the setter starts to the right and behind her outside hitter who is playing in the front court. Whenever the setter is in the back court during the serve, she is not allowed to have her feet in front of the passers in the front court. This may vary somewhat, depending on the rotation, but for now it holds true.

After the server makes contact with the ball, the setter runs as fast as she can to the primary setting position. During the flight of the ball, as she is running to her spot, her eyes are fixed on the ball and its target. As soon as she and the ball cross, she turns her head and the rest of her body with a hop to the setting position. The hop will balance her body and get her ready to set the ball. She must always turn and face her entire team so she can see everyone, even though her eyes are fixed on the passer.

After she has made the set and covers the hitter, she must then run back to position 1 and get ready for defense — if the ball is dug by the opponent.

Second Rotation

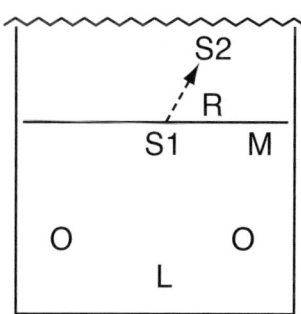

The second rotation takes the setter to the middle back or position 6. In this rotation the setter should go all the way up to the 10-foot line or even to the net, as long as she keeps the middle- and right-side hitters in front of her. Also, the player in position

5 must stay to her left, but these rotations will vary depending on what your coach's strategy and the location of your best passers.

As soon as contact is made from the server, the setter takes a quick two-step with a hop, body facing the team and ready to set. If the ball stays in play she must now get off the net and hurry to her defensive position.

Third Rotation

The setter is in position 5 in the third rotation. Again, the safest place for her is behind and to the right of the middle who is in the left front position. The setter must make sure that everyone else is to her right.

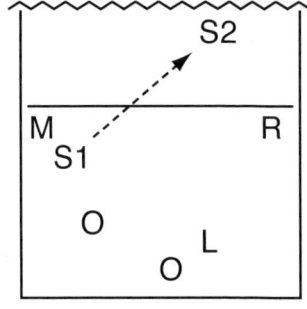

When the server makes contact with the ball, the setter runs in a straight line to her spot. As the ball crosses her, her body starts to turn and again, the last two steps will be a hop with her body facing the team and her back slightly to her opponents.

Fourth Rotation

The setter is in position 4 for the fourth rotation. She is now on the net, which means her job is much easier because she has less ground to cover to reach her spot. She should make sure, though, that she is not ahead of anyone and that she is the closest to the net. She should move

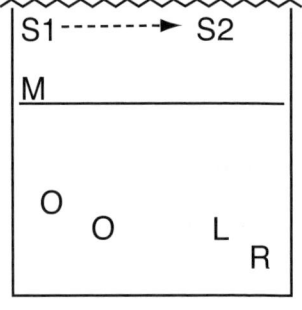

in a straight line and turn her body as soon as the ball crosses the net. Then she hops to her spot and watches how the ball is passed before she makes her next move.

Fifth Rotation

The fifth rotation is even easier because the setter is now two feet from her setting spot and can set up the ball without having to move too much. Here she doesn't have to worry about overlapping with anyone except the middle who is in position 2. She should just make sure that the middle is the closest to the sideline.

The setter needs to keep her back turned slightly to her opponents, with her left leg behind and her head turned to the server. She watches the ball as it travels to her passers. The only running she has to do will come from a bad pass.

Sixth Rotation

The sixth rotation is the easiest, because the setter is now standing in her primary spot and she doesn't have to worry about overlapping with anyone. Her body position and motion are the same as in rotation 5.

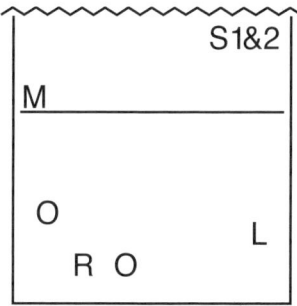

As the setter, always remember where you go after the ball is set — whether you are in the front or back court. Remember to call your set so that you and your hitters know what to do, and cover after you have made your choice. Be very vocal and clear so that everyone understands you, and always know what works best for you and your team.

Types of Sets

All of the different sets can be effective in a game, but when and how you use them is what separates the good setters from the great. Some of the most popular sets are used because they are the only set the setter knows or the only sets she makes consistently to the same spot. Some setters will always choose to set the best hitter. Coaches must be aware of this so that the setter doesn't become trapped and unable to make any other sets.

The most common sets in high school, college and even adult volleyball are listed below. There are also many combination plays, but in this section we will only describe the two most common, the X and the Split Set.

1. High Ball Outside
2. Front One
3. Back One
4. Shoot Set to Outside
5. Short Shoot or 31 Set
6. Back Three or Four)
7. Back Court A-B-C
8. X
9. Split Set
10. Slide Set
11. Setter's Tip

1. High Ball Outside

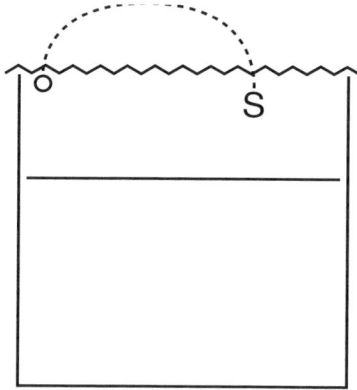

The setter sets the ball from the right side of the court, near the net, high in the air so that it comes down on the left side, right in front of the outside hitter. The ball should reach seven to 10 feet above the net and one to two feet in from the net. If the ball were to fall to the floor, it would land about one foot outside the sideline. All setters should try to master this set because it is commonly used and can often get you out of a tough situation. But even though this is one of the safest and easiest sets to make, it should only be used when you have a good outside hitter and the opponent has a small blocker.

Because of the ball's height in this set, if it falls short of the outside and comes down in the middle of the court, the hitter has time to make the adjustment and still get a kill. This makes it look like a good set. The height of the High Ball Outside also gives the hitter enough time to see where the blockers are heading and to hit elsewhere.

With this set, the hitter should have at least five options for hitting the ball in order to get the kill: cross court, down the line, off the blockers' hands (which we'll talk about more in the chapter on hitting), the tip over the blockers, and the hit over the blockers, if you can hit high enough. After the set is made you must ask yourself whether your hitter had these choices. Take a minute next time to ask her.

A good time to set the ball to the outside is when there is a short blocker matched against your best hitter. Another time is when you freeze the middle blocker, meaning that the middle blocker has moved to the middle of the net, expecting the hit to come across there, and then has no time to get to the outside to help with that block. Consequently, you end up with just one blocker on the outside.

Also, when you get a pass that takes you all the way over to the right side of the court, think about setting to the outside. Most setters will set this ball to the middle or the back court and most blockers know this. If you are strong enough, surprise them and push the set to the outside hitter. Now you have the blockers chasing the ball to the outside, and most of the time they will get there late.

2. Front One to Middle

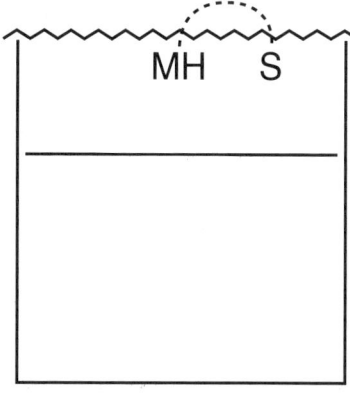

MH   S

This refers to a ball that is set one foot above the net in the middle of the court. This set is released more quickly than the High Ball Outside and is more of a touch and release than a push. This is a quick ball where the middle hitter goes straight to the setter and jumps just as the setter is about to make contact with the ball. It is up to the setter to put the ball in the hitter's hand with a quick flick of the wrist and no follow-through.

With this set, the setter needs to make sure her body is facing the hitter. If her left shoulder is pointing toward the hitter, she won't be able to see the hitter without turning her head. While a setter usually takes a step with her left foot toward the ball, she doesn't with this set in order to keep her left shoulder away from the hitter.

For this set you really want to jump set, especially if you are a short setter, because the ball will clear the top of the net much more quickly and speed up the offense. Since the MH will need to jump for her hit, forcing her to wind up in advance, this action can alert the blockers to the planned hit. With experience, a good setter can see this and change the set at the last minute. This will give your other hitters one-on-one opportunity with a blocker, or sometimes no blockers, as you will see when we describe combination sets.

With a jump set, your footwork will sometimes change depending on where the middle is coming from. Once you can jump set, however, the hitter's direction won't really matter. Remember that a good blocker can tell where a setter is directing the ball by watching her feet and body position.

The Front One should be one of the first sets used in a game. Showing the other team that you have a strong middle who can hit will draw their attention to that spot on the court, freeing up your outside and opposite hitters to make the kills from their positions on the court. It's a "freezer set," meaning that you can freeze the blockers away from your other hitters.

3. Back One

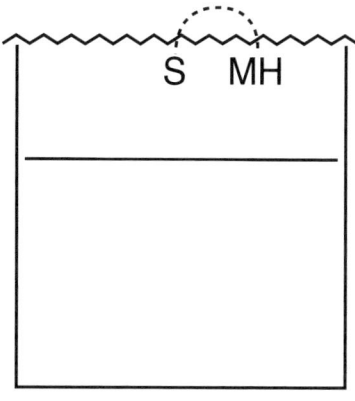

In this set, the ball has the same tempo as the Front One, but is set about one foot high and right behind the setter's head. The setter still steps into the ball with her left foot and squares her body, but after the ball is released, the follow-through with the left leg takes her body forward slightly. The height should be the same and you must have a feel for the hitter. Again, if the hitter likes the ball at two or two-and-a-half feet rather than one foot, the setter should know this and adjust accordingly.

For this set, the setter is *not* working to put the ball in the hitter's hand; she is setting to a specific spot. She has a slight backward lean on the release of the ball, and a quick flick of the wrists instead of an extension of the arms.

Most of the time, the middle blocker position will dictate where your setter sets the ball, so before she takes off, she should be able see her hitter and the blocker in the middle. The setter's eyes must be moving all the time, but she should never move her head to look. A glance is all she should need to see whether the middle blockers are ready to jump. If they are, she shouldn't set the middle because it's one of the easiest sets to block. The ball is much closer to the net, and it's more difficult for your hitter to find an angle that works for the hit. If there's a middle blocker who can close or cover these angles, she will.

4. Shoot Set to the Outside

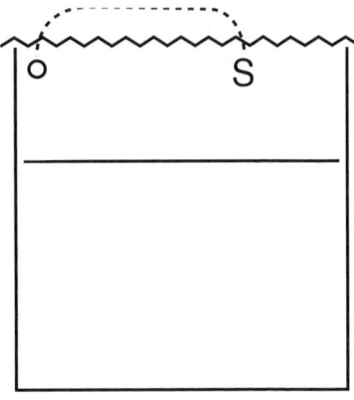

A shoot refers to a ball that travels across the court at a fast speed. A Shoot Set to the Outside is a quick ball that is pushed across the court, one to two feet above the net, sometimes higher depending on your hitter. The Shoot Set should end up in front of the outside hitter, right by the antenna on the outside or left side of the net.

To set a Shoot Set, the setter's position is the same as the high set, with the left foot toward the ball and the right foot facing the target. The difference comes when the setter releases the ball. Her hands should finish the set six to 10 inches lower than they would for a high outside set. If you were to draw a line from your setter's hands to the antenna, the hitter would make contact with the ball where the line intersects the antenna. And when the ball arrives at your hitter, she should have the same five options for hitting the set. Some setters will jump set the ball so that the Shoot Set travels in a straight line. If she can jump and reach the ball and release it so that it travels a foot or two above the net, then there would be no arc to the ball.

A Shoot Set is used when you are trying to match up your hitters one on one with the blockers. Most of the time, there will only be one blocker in front of your hitter, be-

---

After the setter releases the ball, she must cover her hitter. She is the only one on the team who knows where the ball is going before the set is made, so she should be the first to cover in case the ball is blocked.

cause the set is so fast that the middle blocker will not get there in time. If executed correctly, it is a very effective set, but it is also one that requires a lot of time and work between the setter and hitter. It's also not a popular set in high school because it is a high-risk set. Sometimes the ball will be too low, too fast, too high, too much inside or outside, or the hitter is too early or too late. With so much room for error, this set is not used very often.

5. Short Shoot or 31 Set

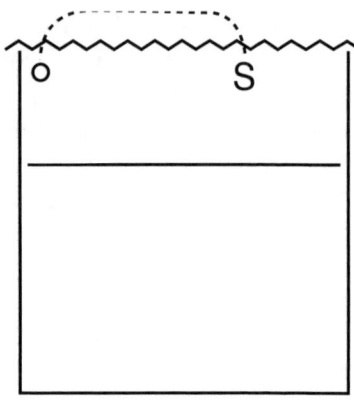

This set takes good timing. The tempo is the same as the Back One, and the ball is set with a pushing motion. But this set rises only one-and-a-half to two feet above the net and travels only half-way across the court. If the ball were to drop, it would drop near the middle of the court.

The setter's job here, as with the Front One and the Back One, is to put the ball in the hitter's hand. In other words, the hitter must be up in the air so the setter can send the ball directly to her. Again the footwork is the same, and the hands finish as the Shoot Set. The only difference here is that the ball is pushed less because the setter is only pushing approximately four feet in front of her, not 15 to get it across the court.

This set is used to split the blockers and force them to move out of their comfort zone. It should be used if your opponent's middle blocker is very big and very good at blocking.

6. Back Three or Four

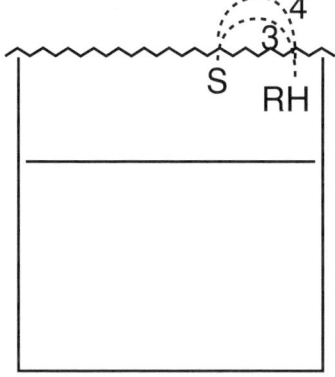

This is a set that sends the ball behind the setter toward the antenna. It is not as high as the High Ball Outside but should be high enough to give the hitter a chance to make any adjustments she needs. The footwork is basic but the ball is released to the back.

The ball must be set overhead, but it should look like it is being set over the right shoulder. The setter needs to rotate her right shoulder back just as or after she releases the ball. This rotation takes the body toward the net and the ball away from the net, and it also helps position the setter for her next move, which is covering the hitter. A very experienced setter will set directly over her head with little or no bending of the back and the set will be perfect. But in the beginning, she must make sure she steps with her left foot first and finishes with her arms extended fully toward her target as she rotates to her right to cover.

The common problem with this set is that the ball sometimes shoots past the antenna because there is too much arch in the setter's back. If there is not enough arch, the ball goes straight up and not out, or the ball goes too close to the net and sometimes into the antenna. And if the setter turns or rotates to the left, it takes the ball into the net.

7. Back Court A-B-C

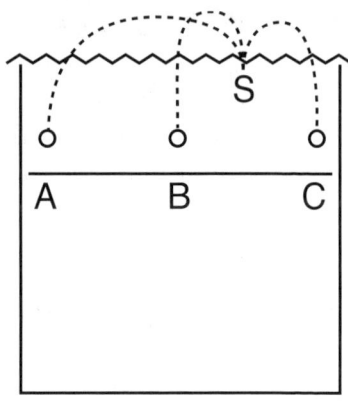

It is called a back-court set because the ball is hit by a player in the back court even though the ball must be set in front of the 10-foot line. How close you want to set the ball to the net is based on the person hitting the ball. The hitter must jump or take off behind the 10-foot line, and no part of her feet should touch the line until after contact is made with the ball. She can land in front of the line.

The body position, the footwork, the height of release and follow through for this set are the same for the High Ball Outside. The only difference here is that the right foot points away from the net a few degrees. This foot will determine how far off the net you will make the set, and with experience, this will not matter too much.

Make sure the ball is at least three feet inside the 10-foot line. The body stays in the same position as if you were setting the outside. That way you don't give away your target.

Most of the time, a back court set is used in a combination play. The back court player lines up with the A position on the outside, the B position in the middle (which is sometimes called the "Pipe"), and the C position behind the setter.

The best time to set the A is when you pull your outside hitter in for a quick play which forces her blocker to move toward the middle of the court, leaving the outside line open.

The Pipe or B is set when the opponent's middle blocker is so effective that every time your MH jumps, the MB jumps. At that point you can surprise everyone with a quick Pipe that is lower than the other two back court sets. It must be lower and quick because you don't want the MB to land on the floor and jump again. With the MB landing while your MH is hitting, she'll have more court to hit instead of sharp angles. In the B set, everything is the same, except the ball is released more to the left side of the face and the hands finish straight up, with the ball falling right behind the middle hitter.

The C is a back set that is not as high as an outside set, but not as low as a Pipe set. It's somewhere in the middle. This set is more effective when the setter calls a play that also takes the right-side hitter to the middle of the court for a combination play. Most of the time will force the blocker to come inside and block, opening up the right side of the court. These sets, even though they might be to your best hitters, are sometimes not your best choice.

In the C set, the body and footwork are the same as the back set except the ball is released over the left side of the face with the same rotation.

> **You never want to set the Back Court A when there is an outside hitter in the outside position, because it will cause confusion as to whose ball it is. Never set the B or Pipe if the middle blocker did not jump, and never set the C if you have your right-side hitter back there.**

8. X

The X set is intended to confuse the blockers. As a setter, you have to see who or which blocker jumps, then choose to whom you will set the ball — your middle or your opposite hitter, also called the right-side hitter.

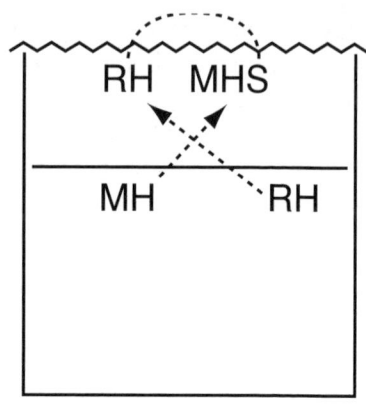

What makes this combination play an X is the crossing of these two players. The most common X play is where the opposite hitter, on the right side, comes to the middle of the court and crosses behind the middle hitter. She then hits a ball that is set slightly higher and to the left shoulder of the middle hitter. The X can also come from the outside, where the outside hitter comes into the middle of the court and hits a two ball slightly higher than the middle set. You can also run an X on a 31 Set with the right-side player, but your best choice would be to set a Back Court C because with this X you are jamming all the blockers to the left side of the court and no one will be over there to challenge the set.

This play is a good choice when you see that your opponent's middle blocker jumps with the middle hitter. If the middle blocker does not jump, you need to identify that and set the ball to the MH. Later when we look at blocking, you will see how to block against these sets.

9. Split Set

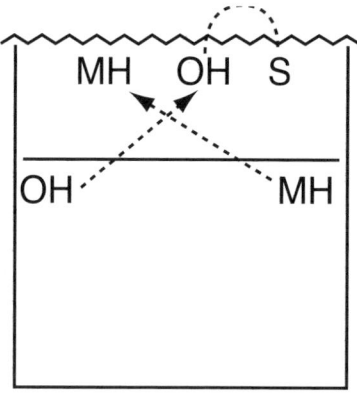

The Split Set is similar to the X except it is a much quicker set where the outside hitter or the right-side hitter comes between the middle and the setter. It uses only a Short Shoot or Front One toward the middle of the court. With this combination, you might want to set the Back Court A, Pipe or C. It depends on which hitter is coming around to hit the middle.

As a setter, you don't call either of these two combination plays just because they look fancy. These plays should be used to confuse your opponent, and for every combination play, there is a more effective play to make. Your choice of plays is actually determined by how effectively your opponents are blocking.

10. Slide Set

The Slide Set is a quick back set behind the setter to the antenna. With this set, the setter calls the middle to the center of the court, but instead of setting a Front or Back One, the setter sets the ball away from the middle and back toward the antenna. The middle, from the center of the court, quickly drops back from the net and runs around the setter. Then she jumps off the left leg as she attacks the ball.

There are two other ways to run the slide. Instead of going toward the setter, the middle hitter can go in a straight line toward the ball and the antenna, or go along the 10-foot line and then turn toward the ball and at the antenna.

The footwork and body position are the same as the back set except the ball is released lower than the regular set. Some hitters pefer speed where they have to chase the ball before it gets too far and some hitters prefer height. A setter should know her hitters and their perferences. See Chapter 6 for more information on hitting a slide.

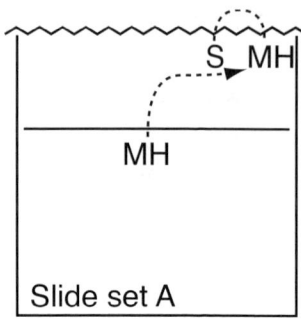

Slide set A

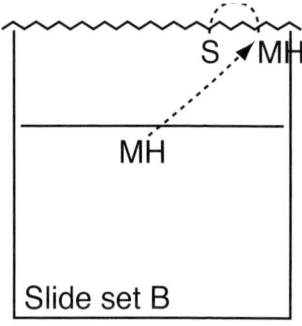

Slide set B

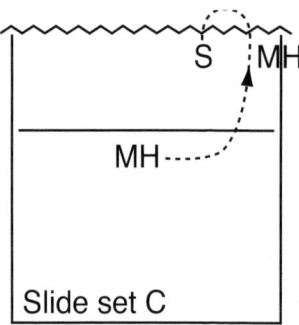

Slide set C

11. Setter's Tip

The Setter's Tip is a quick left-handed push of the ball over the net when the opponent is expecting a set. The setter should appear to be setting the ball but at the last moment, the left hand comes over the right and pushes the ball to the floor. Before you tip you must know where the open spot is and how to get the ball there as quickly as possible.

Tipping for a setter starts with a high jump. The higher you can jump, the higher you can reach above the net and the harder or more quickly you can get the ball to the floor. If you can't get that height over the net, then the wrist is used. With a quick flick of the wrist to the open spot, the ball will get there just as fast. All of this will come with time and hard work.

The left hand tip, where hands start out like a set or overhead pass

A Word on Jumping

Great jumpers are born, not made, and your genes and genetic make-up contribute a big part to how high you can actually jump. But everyone can learn and train to be a faster, higher jumper, and I'll talk more about this in the chapter on hitting, as well as give you exercises to improve your jumping skills.

A Final Word on Setting

It makes sense that if you have a really strong hitter, you set to her wherever she is on the court, especially if the game is close or you really need a side out. Setting a ball in the back court when she is there might fool the offense, but it is not always the best play, because you might not get your strongest hit from that position. Plus, the other team will be expecting you to set to this star player.

It's okay to "reset" a player when she makes a mistake on her hit. It shows her that you have confidence in her hitting ability and helps her move along her game.

The Setting Tree

I came up with the chart below that tells you the *how, why, when* and *where* of setting. The how has to do with the basics of the sets. You have to know *how* to set each set first before you can use them in a game. The *why* deals with the choices you must make. The hitters determine *when* to use the different sets, and the *where* looks at the ball and where you are sending it.

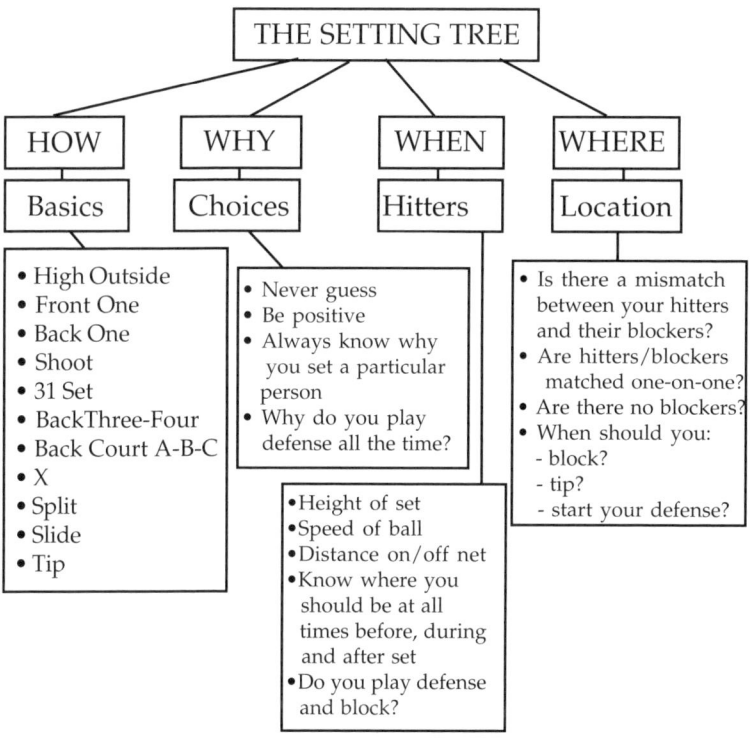

THE SETTING TREE

HOW — Basics
- High Outside
- Front One
- Back One
- Shoot
- 31 Set
- BackThree-Four
- Back Court A-B-C
- X
- Split
- Slide
- Tip

WHY — Choices
- Never guess
- Be positive
- Always know why you set a particular person
- Why do you play defense all the time?

- Height of set
- Speed of ball
- Distance on/off net
- Know where you should be at all times before, during and after set
- Do you play defense and block?

WHEN — Hitters

WHERE — Location
- Is there a mismatch between your hitters and their blockers?
- Are hitters/blockers matched one-on-one?
- Are there no blockers?
- When should you:
  - block?
  - tip?
  - start your defense?

4 Serving: Your Best Weapon

Whether you're looking for power or precision, serving is your first and best offensive weapon. A good serve – one that is hard to pass – and its accompanying ace, can rack up some points at the start of a game, throwing your opponent off base. It can stack up some points in the middle of the game, changing the balance of the game. And it can cinch a victory with a sweet taste.

But who hasn't been on the line with the score tied, match point, and served into the net. It happens to the best of us in every sport. Baseball players strike out. Basketball players miss the hoop. So don't dwell on it. Go practice instead.

You probably have a good serve now, but I want to teach you how to have a great serve. If you are a shorter girl, you have an opportunity here to polish a skill that will put you on the team and get you in the game. Let's start with the basics of the float serve.

The Float Serve

The float serve is the most common serve at all levels of volleyball, and while it is somewhat easy to do, it's very difficult to master. It is called the float because the ball appears to float over the net, rather than spin at a faster speed. Because this serve is not a power serve, it's important to learn to control where it goes. You will know when you have mastered a float serve – with the proper control and technique, you will be able to send it to any spot on the court.

The Set-Up

Many girls have a routine before they serve the ball, whether they bounce the ball three or five times on the floor or twirl it or spin it in the nonserving hand. However, this is a bad habit to adopt mainly because it takes time. Once the whistle blows, you have only six seconds to serve the ball, and if you bounce it or spin it for four seconds, you're leaving yourself only two seconds to position the ball and make contact.

One reason, however, that people spin and bounce the ball is to locate and place the valve on the volleyball. The valve is the heaviest part of the ball, and when you hit the ball, it will go in the direction of the valve. If you turn the valve so that it is facing the floor, the ball will drop more quickly. If you have the valve facing out, the ball will go straight. If the valve is to the left, the ball will eventually bear left, and with the valve to the right, the ball will eventually go right.

But before you concern yourself with the position of the valve and think that you can depend on it to serve to a specific spot, you need to learn to serve perfectly, over and over, every time. For now, concentrate on hitting the ball squarely on the ball's logo, with the valve on the opposite side, facing the other court.

The Stance

To learn the float serve or to review what you already know, stand with your weight on your back leg, your dominant leg. The opposite leg from your serving arm is in front and is relaxed. Your toes are pointed toward your target. Your serving arm is bent at the elbow and your forearm is parallel to the floor and a little higher than your shoulder. Your wrist is firm. Your other arm is stretched out in front, slightly bent, holding the ball. This arm is across your chest slightly, toward your hitting arm.

Ready position for float serve and height of toss

After you have chosen where you want to serve the ball, your eyes then stay on the ball at all times. If you look to the other side of the court after the toss or before you make contact with the ball, you're in trouble.

And here goes the toss...

Stop right there! Let the ball fall to the floor five to 10 inches in front of your front leg after the step, and keep your serving arm bent at the elbow, ready to hit the ball. Now toss the ball again and look at it this time. Your toss should be one to two feet into the air. Now toss the ball again and let it drop to the floor. And again. To have an effective serve, you MUST have a consistent toss. Toss it a few more times.

Pictured at the right is where the ball should land if you let it drop from your toss.

The Toss

Let's examine the toss more closely by looking at the hand that is tossing the ball. The ball should sit on the upper pads of the palm of your hand, just below where your fingers start. If it sits in the palm of your hand, you'll get spin on the ball after the toss. If the ball sits too high on your fingers, you'll have less control.

Here's how to grip the ball before the toss.

Now toss with your entire arm, not just your wrist, so that the ball just floats up from your hand. The toss should be vertical. A long, slow lift is better than a short, quick action, and don't bend your wrist. Bending your wrist or following through on the toss will send the ball flying over your head.

Note how it feels when you make a good toss and a bad toss. When you make a bad toss, check your position.

Hand Contact

After you've checked the valve and mastered your stance and the toss, the next step in serving is hitting the ball. Only you will be able to know the best place to contact the ball, but generally, once you toss it, you want to hit it after it stops ascending and before it starts descending. Shorter girls need to make contact with the ball at a point that is a little higher than that for tall girls, so you may need to stretch or go up on your toes a little. Whatever your height, you must be able to see the top of the net as you hit the ball. One way to check is to stand where you normally serve and ask your coach or a teammate to hold the ball in front of you at the height where you can see the top of the net under the ball. Or you can hold the ball with two hands, and when you can see the top of the net underneath the ball, you'll know where you'll need to contact the ball.

Most people's reach is one-and-a-half to two feet above their shoulders. How far you reach and where you make contact is up to you, but somewhere in there you want to hit the ball firmly and squarely with the thick portion of your hand.

Hand contact for the float serve: Notice where the hand makes contact on the ball. Note that the fingers are off the ball and pointing up toward the ceiling.

Serving drill for the float serve: This teaches the height of contact from ready position. Hand moves toward the ball with the arm fully extended.

Hand contact: When contact is made, body weight is transferred from back leg to front leg. Contact is made with the meaty portion of the hand and a firm wrist.

Here are three ways to help you make contact with the ball:

1. Hold the ball on a wall with your nonhitting hand. Keep your body in the serving position. Hit the ball in the serving motion while holding it on the wall at the highest point in the serve. Do this 10-20 times without moving the ball.

2. Gently hit the ball off a wall at the height of contact for your serve. The point of this drill is to practice making contact with the ball and the wall, not to smack the ball on the wall. So hit it softly against the wall, starting from 10 feet away and increasing to 20 feet.

3. Have your partner hold the ball exactly where you make contact with it. Go through the serving motion, from the ready position to the middle position with your arms extended fully, and then to the contact position with your bodyweight transferred from your back leg to your front leg.

Hitting the Ball

As you toss the ball, your serving arm rotates at the shoulder, with your forearm rotating backward at the elbow. As you are about to make contact with the ball, move your forearm and hitting hand up and forward. You should hit the ball directly above and in front of your hitting shoulder. When you make contact with the ball, hit it with the lower two-thirds of the palm of your hand. Your palm should be flat, your fingers spread wide and pointing to the ceiling, and your forearm and elbow should form a straight line. The tighter the connection from your wrist to your forearm, the harder you'll hit the ball. You want this tight connection so that all of the pressure from the hit goes into the ball.

Hitting the ball: Notice the extension of the body and arm and the weight on the front foot. The elbow is locked, the head is up and the eyes are looking at the ball.

There is no follow-through after hitting the ball, either with your arms or your legs, except for a little drag with the foot that matches your hitting arm. If you follow through with your legs, your body will rotate and the ball will curve.

The goal in serving is to make contact with the ball in the same place every time. Don't swing fast or rush or you'll develop bad habits which will send the ball into the net or off to the side. Here's a line to help you remember this:

Check yourself before you wreck yourself. Feet. Knees. Hips. Body weight. Wrist. Fingers. Elbows. Shoulders. Head. Eyes.

Here's a drill for accuracy: Serve to each of the six positions on the court. Put a towel on each spot on the court and try to aim the ball to hit the towel. Some players like to put chairs in the back court to try to hit, but if you hit the chairs, you may be serving outside the line. Plus, towels decrease the chance of fly-away balls.

Eye on the Ball

You always want to see the ball when you hit it. If you step under the ball to hit it, you won't be able to see it. When you're learning to serve, start by serving from five feet behind the net. Then work your way to the middle of the court, and then to the back line, and then five feet behind the back line. Serve from each spot about 20 times.

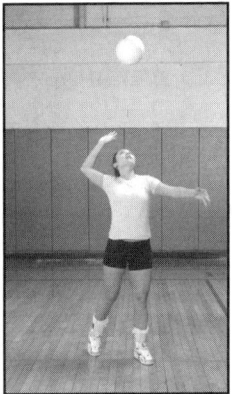  

Float Serve: Notice the height of the toss, the height of contact, and contact on the center of the ball. As eyes stay fixed on the ball, body weight transfers from the back to the front leg on contact and the serving hand stays in the air, with fingers pointed to the ceiling after contact is made. There is no follow-through with either the hitting or serving hand.

Notice how the entire palm makes contact with the ball for a Top Spin serve. Compare this to how the meaty part of the hand makes contact at the center of the ball for a float serve.

Top Spin Serve

A top spin serve, which is more powerful than the float serve, sends the ball in a straight line with more speed than the float and a good deal of spin at the same time. Balls with top spin are easier to pass, so you should serve a top spin away from a good passer and never to the zero spot on to court, which is dead center between the 6 and 3 positions. The zero spot is the easiest part of the court to pass from, because each passer can take one step and still keep their passing platform straight. There's no change in body position. If you're going to serve to the zero spot, make sure it's a hard driven ball, like a hard jump serve or a float serve that falls closer to the 10-foot line than the center of the court. The middle back passer will pass the top spin serve 90% of the time because it is just a straight line from her to the setter.

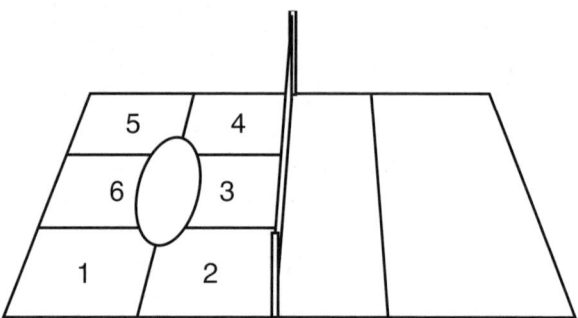

The zero spot on the court

To get an effective spin on the ball, you should stand as you would for a float serve, but toss the ball a little higher in the air, give it a flick of the wrist to get some forward spin, and toss it a little more in front of your serving shoulder. When you make contact with the ball, follow through with a snap of the wrist, folding your fingers over the ball. Make sure your fingers are spread out and your wrist is loose, not stiff, and you contact the ball with the palm of your hand.

Contact for a top spin serve: Contact should be made at least two feet above the head and in front of the serving shoulder. Note how the hand curls over the ball for this serve.

There's also a little bit more follow-through with your back leg on a top spin serve. This follow-through looks like a step toward the line and adds more body weight into the serve.

Ready position for the top spin serve: one-handed toss

Body leans back in spiking motion

Weight transfers from back to front after contact

A shorter server needs to follow through more with her wrist than her arm. If she follows through with her arm, she will pull the ball down below the top of the net, whereas a taller server may still make it over the net.

79

In the final phase, note the downward motion of the wrist as the left hand crosses the stomach.

Practice serving the ball over the net from five feet behind the net, from ten feet behind the net, from the back court line, and then beyond the back line, just as you did for the float serve, using either the towels or chairs.

Here's a drill that teaches you the right speed for contact: Put a line of tape on a wall at the height of the net. Then put the sequence together – the stance, toss and contact and hit the ball so that it comes straight back to you. Pick a spot on the wall that is one foot over the net line and aim for it. But don't concentrate on hitting the ball on the wall. Instead, concentrate on your serving motion on each part of the serving process you've learned.

Here's a drill for getting top spin on the ball: Hit the ball against a wall so that the ball bounces forward, hits the wall and comes back to you. The ball must make contact with the wall above the marker (a line of tape) that represents the top of the net. Adjust your hitting power and distance from the wall so that the ball comes back directly to you. Then attack the ball with a serving motion, using a loose wrist, fingers spread wide and a snapping motion.

Drill for the top spin serve: Have your partner hold the ball as high as possible. Here, the server is in the tossing phase. Elbows are very high. Go through all the body motions for the top spin serve and pay special attention to where you contact the ball that your partner is holding. Notice how your hand curls over the ball on contact and your body is extended for higher contact.

Remember: Spin to No One Special

Never serve a top spin serve directly to a receiver. Aim the serve to the space between the receivers.

The Jump Serve

To hit a jump serve properly, you need to approach the ball as if you're spiking. The difference is that you are tossing the ball yourself rather than having a setter set it to you. Before you start practicing the jump serve, you should master a float and top spin serve, as well as your hitting skills, or you will be trying to crack a coconut without an axe.

As you begin to practice a jump serve, you need to find your sweet spot behind the serving line. To do this, stand at the back court line and take three or four steps, whichever is more comfortable for you, away from the court and jump. Have someone mark your take-off spot with a piece of tape and then turn around and start your serving approach from the tape. As long as you don't touch the back line during take-off, it's okay to land inside the court after you've made contact with the ball.

With a jump serve, the ball is tossed higher than the other serves, somewhere between 10 and 15 feet, and it is tossed in front of your approach. It takes a lot of practice to achieve this part consistently. Practice tossing as much as you can, because your toss will determine the power and effectiveness of your serves.

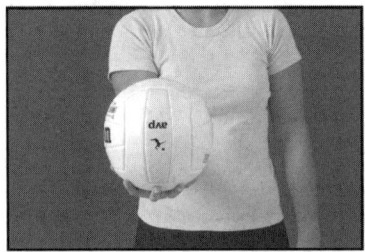 

Front and side view of the proper way to hold the ball for a jump serve with a one-handed toss

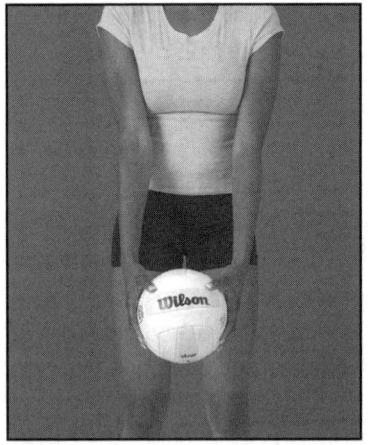 

Front and side view of the proper way to hold the ball for a jump serve with a two-handed toss

Toss the ball a few times and see where it lands. It should land at least one foot into the court. If you can make contact with the ball more than a foot into the court and still keep it legal, more power to you!

When you practice your jump serve, start from 10 feet behind the net with the toss, approach, jump and hit, and then move back 20 feet from the net with the toss, approach, jump and hit, and finally from your regular serving spot.

Jump serve drill: Practice your jump serve without the ball until you get very comfortable on your approach. Then add the ball, but instead of hitting it, catch it at the highest point of your jump. Notice where you are landing at all times because this can also help you determine how far in the court you're tossing the ball.

Tossing the Ball

It doesn't matter whether you toss the ball with one hand or two. Both have their advantages and disadvantages. If you choose to toss with one hand but don't have a good grip on the ball, you may lose the ball during the tossing stage, resulting in a bad toss that may then lead to a serving error. It may be easier to start with a two-handed toss, although this toss might not have much forward spin, and if you hold it too tightly it will affect your release and may not be consistent.

Essentially, you're going to toss the ball high in the air, make the approach, wind up for the jump, then jump and swing. After you swing and land, you should run to the court and get ready for defense. This takes a lot of practice, and it's very important to coordinate your toss with your approach. Sometimes you have a bad toss, and if the toss is low, you'll need to get a quick jump on the ball as you'll

VOLLEYBALL

Ready position for jump serve with one-handed toss: Notice the complete follow-through of the tossing hand and the arms finishing higher than the shoulders to create more height on the toss.

Feet plant in pigeon-toed position. Body lifts in a backwards "C" position. The entire motion is the same as spiking.

have very little time to make adjustments to keep the ball in play. If your toss is too high, you will have to wait a little before starting your approach, and you'll have some time to make a correction. Beach volleyball players toss it low because the wind will carry the ball in another direction.

Contact the ball and follow through, as the nonserving arm wraps around the body.

Shorter girls who master the jump serve show the other team that they are not only smart, but powerful. Mastering a jump serve also shows your coach that what you lack in height, you make up for in drive. So go for it — after you perfect your other serves!

Ready position for the two-handed toss for jump or top spin serve and the one-handed toss for the top spin or float serve.

The Jump Float

The purpose of the jump float is to hit the ball in a straight line over the net and down into your opponent's court. The ball travels much faster and sometimes will carry out of bounds. The approach is the same as that of the jump serve, except you have a much shorter distance for your approach and the contact is the same as the float serve. Also, the jump is not as explosive. It's better to use a two-handed toss here because you don't want spin on the ball. The jump and the toss happen at the same time, and the toss should be about four feet, with contact at the highest point.

Other Serves

There are a few other serve such as the underarm float and the round house or Chinese floater serve. I don't teach the underarm serve because at a middle school or high school level, you should be concentrating on a Float serve. Plus, an underarm serve is like giving the opponent a free ball.

With the other serve, the round house or Chinese floater, you stand sideways and serve the ball over your head so the competition can't see where it's coming from. This serve is very difficult to master because of the body position and movement of the arm. This serve is used mainly by very experienced players.

Aces Up Your Sleeves

There are several factors that combine to give you an ace. Aces on a jump serve are more common because of the speed and spin on the ball, but you can increase the odds of an ace on a float serve if you pay attention to where and to whom you are sending the ball. Your coach has a better idea of the formation of the team on the other side of the net and can signal you with his or her idea of where to serve the ball. Depending on this information, he or she should tell you whether to use a float serve or a top spin serve. This will be discussed in more detail in the chapter on the specialists.

It's important to learn the different serves, because not every receiver can pass every kind of serve. While a receiver might be great at passing a float serve, she may have trouble passing a top spin serve. And most girls in high school have difficulty passing a jump serve.

Building Your Serving Strength

Serving a volleyball puts a lot of stress on the shoulder joint because of the force you must exert to get the ball to go the distance. You need a strong shoulder and proper technique to create speed and velocity in the serve, and with this combination, you will reduce the risk of injury. Also to avoid injury, you should take time to warm up and stretch out your shoulder muscles before and after practice. Working with resistance bands is a good way to strengthen your shoulders.

Using resistance bands to build shoulder strength will give you a stronger serve and help prevent shoulder injuries.

Resistance bands can be tied to a sturdy wall or post. Don't tie it to a doorknob or something that can pull loose. Pull the band toward you in a serving motion 30-40 times. Do this every other day, giving your shoulder muscles a day to rest.

Another good exercise to build shoulder muscles and increase serving strength is to toss a medicine ball. Medicine balls start at 2 pounds and go up in weight from there.

Tossing the medicine ball over your head: Notice the footwork and extension of the arms. With a teammate, toss a medicine ball from over your head with two hands. Start with your feet together and step as you toss. Follow through completely with your arms. Then toss with one hand in a serving or spiking motion, and finally, toss it from the center of your chest, like a chest pass in basketball. Make sure you step and follow through on all three tosses.

Center chest medicine ball toss: Start with feet together, then step and push, and follow through with the arms.

Conditioning Your Shoulders

Before you practice, whether you're serving, setting or hitting, you should first warm up your shoulder muscles along with other major muscles groups. After practicing, you need to stretch out those same muscles. Remember, you always want to start out with a gradual warm-up and finish with a gentle cool-down.

Warming Up Your Shoulders with a Volleyball

1. Start by tossing the ball off a wall first with your right hand, then with your left hand, and then with both hands.

2. Next, stand with your left shoulder toward the wall and with your right hand toss the ball against the wall, moving your right arm across your chest. Then reverse, starting with your right shoulder toward the wall.

Use the technique here to warm up your shoulders, then turn back to the end of Chapter 2 and use the exercises I outlined for conditioning for the overhead pass to condition and stretch out your shoulders.

Stretching Your Shoulders

Stretching after practice is very important. Start now to make it a regular part of your routine. Here's how:

Across the Chest Stretch

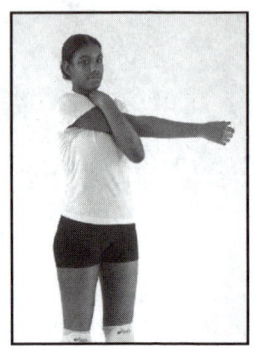

Extend your right arm out straight and place the back of your left hand on the outside of your right elbow. Using your left hand, gently pull your right arm toward the left side of your body. Reverse arms.

Elbow Pull

Extend your right arm up straight from your shoulder and bend your elbow so your hand hangs down toward the center of your back. Gently use your left hand to pull your elbow and upper arm toward your head. Reverse arms.

Shoulder Rotation

Rotate your right shoulder forward and backward a few times. Switch shoulders.

Arm/Floor Stretch

Sit on the floor and stretch your arms behind you with your wrists facing away from you and palms resting on the floor. Gently reach as far back as possible.

Wall Press

Press your left shoulder against a wall with your left arm extended parallel to the floor and turn your face to the right. Gently turn your body to the right. Reverse.

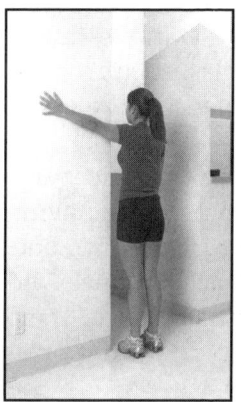 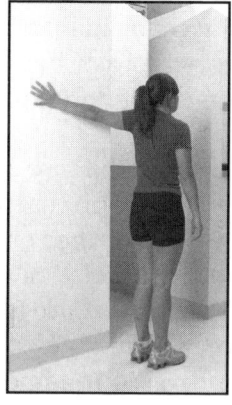 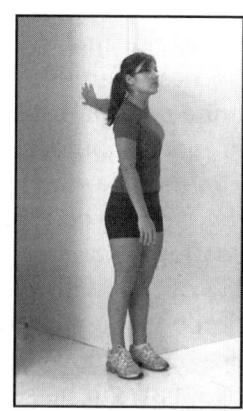

Between the Door Stretch

Bend your elbows on a doorway, step forward with one leg and push your chest forward.

Partner Stretch

Place your hands on your hips with your thumbs forward and have your partner gently squeeze back your elbows. Then extend your arms straight back and have her squeeze your arms together.

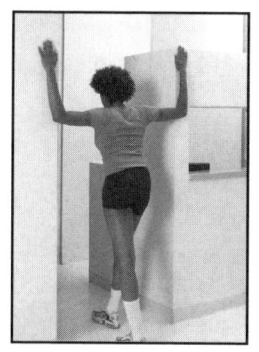

Sore Shoulder

If you overdo your serving practice or strain any of your shoulder muscles, put ice on it right away – 20 minutes on and 20 minutes off for an hour or so. Purchasing a "cold pack" from a medical supply store and leaving it in your freezer so that it is always available is a good investment. You can also use a frozen bag of vegetables, such as peas, but a cold pack will be larger and will balance more easily on your shoulder.

If your shoulder hurts the next day, DON'T practice serving, setting or hitting. Tell your coach that you're having some pain and see a doctor or the trainer if you have one. He or she will tell you what else needs to be done. And don't ever use an injury as an excuse to miss practice. There are other things the coach can give you to do during practice that will help improve your game.

5 Passing: Precision is the Goal

The forearm or underarm pass is used mainly to receive a served ball and to start your offense. It is used almost exclusively when the server really drives the ball or if you have weak fingers. But it can also be used to pass a free ball to the setter, and sometimes by the setter to set a very low passed ball. Its main objective is to stop the ball and redirect it to your target.

Although the basic instruction for the forearm pass sounds simple, it is not the easiest move in volleyball. Often a serve is coming at you hard and fast and your job is not only to stop it, but to send it to a specific place. To do this you need to judge this ball's distance, speed and direction. A lot of that comes with practice, but being ready can be learned.

Body Position

Before the ball is served, your body position should be very relaxed, with shoulders and weight leaning forward a little, knees bent slightly, and arms bent at the elbows. Your feet are moving lightly from side to side with your toes turned out. If you turn your toes out, you will be ready to move toward the ball even faster.

> **To receive a serve, your body must be ready to move more than it must be ready to pass.**

Front and side view of ready position for passing

At the time when the server makes contact with the ball, you want your body's center of gravity to be lower than the ball, and all movement should take place from that lower center of gravity. But when you're waiting for the serve, you want your body to be a little higher. If you're too low before the server makes contact with the ball, you'll need to rise up to move; if you're too high, your first step will be slow. You don't want your body going up and down like a seesaw before you make contact with the ball. Find the spot from which you move forward, back and side to side the fastest, and keep your feet loose and a little wider than your shoulders.

> **Your body is never at complete rest in the ready position for passing.**

The Arms and Hands

As the ball comes over the net, prepare your arms to make contact with the ball. Bring your arms and hands together so that they lock tightly and your wrists point down, and hit the ball with the meaty part of your forearms, between the wrist and elbow. If you look at a picture of penguins clapping their fins, that is how your hands should come together. Never form a "prayer" position with your hands by bending

Correct position of hands and arms for the pass

your elbows and locking your fingers under your chin. Don't start with your arms between your legs either.

In the proper position, your arms pull your shoulders in front of your body, your back is rounded and your body leans forward to help create the angle to pass the ball. How low your body goes to make contact depends on how high the ball has traveled over the net and how short the serve.

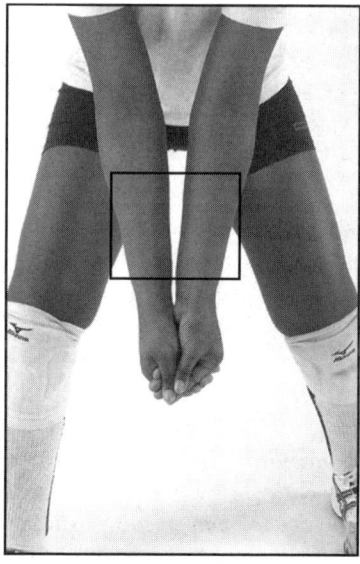

Hand and arm position for passing: Note the box where the ball should make contact on the forearm.

95

The meaty party of the forearm is used to pass the ball because it creates a wide and flat surface for the ball. It's as if your arms turn into a flat board, and the flatter your arms, the better your pass. If you make contact with the bony part of your arms, you won't have as much control of the ball and it will hurt!

From All Angles

To deliver a precision pass, you need to think of your forearms as a flat board. Your legs take your board to the ball, and your arms turn the board to the target, usually your setter. Because volleyball is a rebounding sport, directing the ball from a bounce can be very difficult. If you have the right body position in relation to your location on the court, your job will be much easier.

The different angles of the arms will send the ball in different directions. Here's a good way to see how the angles affect the direction.

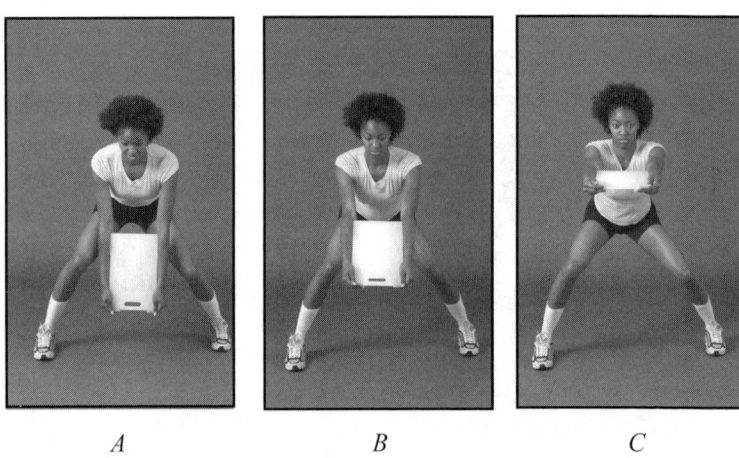

A   B   C

Board drill: These three positions demonstrate the direction in which the ball will go. Picture A is an incorrect position for the arms. If you contact the ball in this position, the ball will go straight down to the floor. Picture B shows the correct position with the board in front of the belly button. Here the ball will go toward the target. In picture C, the ball will go straight up instead of forward.

Stand in the passing position, and hold a piece of 8- by 10-inch flat board by cupping one end of the board with each hand and resting it on the forearms. Raise the board up and down as your partner tosses the ball to it. Watch where the ball goes when you change the angle of the board.

To get the meaty portion of your forearms exposed, it helps to turn your wrists down as far as possible. For the more flexible players, this is a natural position; for others, the following exercise should help.

Exercise for Forearms

To get the best turn-out of your forearms, try these exercises. You should feel the turn-out in your shoulder muscles from all of these positions.

1. Hold a pencil or pen in your hands with your pinkies touching and your palms facing up. Make a fist around the pen or pencil, then straighten your elbows.

2. Bend over from a sitting position, and extend your arms between your legs so that your hands touch your ankles. Squeeze at your knees.

3. Stretch your arm across your chest to loosen your shoulders.

Your Hands

The best way to hold your hands for the forearm pass will vary with each player. Some hand positions give you more support and expose more of your forearms so you should experiment to see which works best for you. Here are some common grips and my opinion of them.

The fist grip: Make a fist with one hand and cover it with the other, pointing both thumbs straight out and down. This grip is weak, and it doesn't give your hands much support to drive the ball. Because there's no support underneath, your hands can come apart. Plus, it doesn't expose your forearms as much as other grips.

  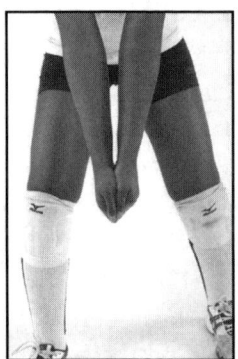

The Fist grip: Front and side view and final position

Interlaced fingers: Each finger intertwines and is again covered by both thumbs pointing out and down. This grip can be slow to come together as the fingers can bump into each other. The ball can also hit a finger and injure it. Although it gives good support, it doesn't expose your forearms to the max.

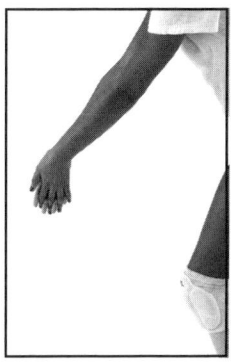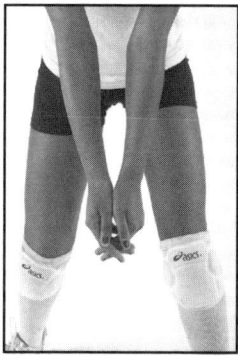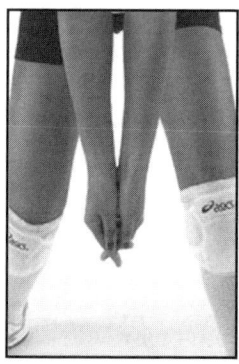

Interlaced fingers grip: Side and front view and final position

Scoop grip: One hand is open with the palm facing up as it grips the other hand, also with the palm facing up, making a "scoop." Thumbs are together and pinch your index finger. This is the most secure grip because the hands are locked and supported by each other with one palm resting on the other. Because both palms are facing up, they expose more of the forearm.

Try to use the scoop grip, but feel free to experiment with others. Just make sure that your hands are gripped tightly so they don't come apart on contact with the ball, and that you are getting the maximum forearm exposure. If you have very little forearm exposure, practice the turn-out exercises and try other grips. Then pick one that is quick and easy to

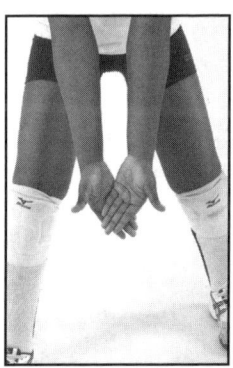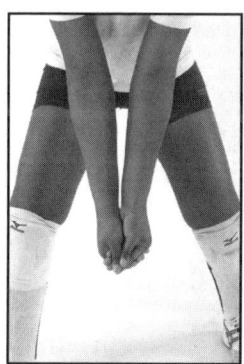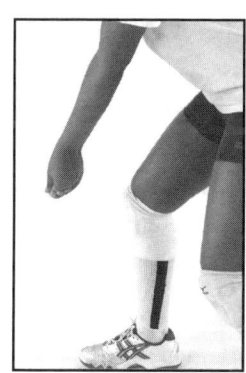

Scoop grip: First position and front and side view

put together and one that stays together when a hard ball comes at you.

Where the Ball Goes

Before the ball is served, fix your eyes on the server and don't let them wander all over the court. It should seem like the entire gym is silent. Early in the game, you should know what kind of ball the server is going to serve to you. You should know this by paying attention to the way each player on the other team serves, and whether they send hard balls with top spin or lofty balls that fall gently.

As the ball leaves the server's hands, your eyes stay on the ball and you begin to call for it if it is coming in your direction. Notice I didn't say if it is coming to you, because sometimes you will have to move to the ball.

As soon as the server makes contact with the ball, your job, especially as a libero or defensive specialist, is to make sure you know where the ball is going before it comes over the net. If you wait until the ball crosses the net, it will be too late. Judging the speed and distance of the ball comes with experience and that is the reason most high school and club coaches use more than three people in serve reception.

Hopping into Position

After you know where the ball is going, you must get there and lower your center of gravity and extend your arms to the spot where the ball is falling. To get to the ball,

Correct hand and arm position for the pass

you must run with your body lower than the ball and get into position to pass. Your last two steps must be a hop to the ball.

On this hop your legs will come apart to balance your body. Your hands come from your sides and lock in your grip. Make sure your

> # Finishing with a hop is the most important part of getting your body into the ready position for passing.

shoulders, your forearms and your feet are facing your target – which is the setter. After contact is made with the ball, your body comes up and you make a slight step forward without changing the angle of your forearms.

Net Balls

Since the ball is now allowed to hit the net on the serve, be prepared for this. If you see the ball coming at the net, have your middle and right-side blockers back up a little and stand at the 10-foot line rather than at the net, because these balls often bounce off the tape and land close to the 10-foot line. These players will get to the ball faster than the passers.

The Give and Take of Passing

As passers, you need to know when to give some forward push to the oncoming serve and when to take away from it. Many people think because the ball is coming so fast and hard that you need to pass it fast and hard. If you return force with force, you will send the ball back over the net to the other team. And if you return soft with soft, your ball might not make it to the setter.

If the ball is served very hard, usually from a hard jump serve, you should take away some of its force as you direct it to your setter. As soon as the ball touches your forearm, pull your arms back a little. Sometimes there's a little backward skip in your step. To do this, you'll need to expose your passing platform to the ball early. Also, don't raise your hands after contact is made with the ball.

If you have a slow serve coming over the net, you must now give some push to the ball. The push comes from the legs, with a follow-through from the back leg that is similar to a little forward step. If you don't give the ball this push, it will not make it to the setter. How much push to give it depends on how far back you are when you're passing, and how slowly the ball comes over the net.

Passing from Your Side

Sometimes a serve will force you to extend your arms to your side or even up to an overhead pass. For this reason, it's important to keep your arms by your side with your elbows bent until you are ready to make contact. Some people wait for the ball as if they are "praying," with their palms together, near their face, with elbows bent. This isn't good. From this position, it will take you too long to get your arms straight and locked in your grip. You need to be in the ready position as the ball clears the net.

The photo on the left, with the left leg in front, shows passing from the left of the back court. This position opens up the body to the court and to the setter who is the target. The picture on the right, with the right leg in front, shows passing from the right side of the back court, again opening the body to the court and to the setter.

The same holds true if your hands are hanging down in front of you. It will take much longer to get up to an overhead pass. Or you'll swing them to the side which, most of the time, will take the ball away from the court and into the bleachers.

Ready position, passing on the right and passing on the left

If your arms are in the correct position for a ball that is off to your side, instead of swinging at the ball you will meet it with a push of your arms. This pushing motion toward the ball is much faster, and you will establish the angle that you need to get the ball to its target. By pushing your arms on the side, you will eliminate the swing motion to the ball.

Remember that even though you are passing from the side, the body's position remains the same as if you were passing in front, and the platform of the forearms must still face its target.

Passing Close to the Net

If you are near the net and need to pass the ball, make sure your platform, the flat surface of your arms, is facing up or starting higher to avoid sending the ball into the net. You need about 12 to 18 inches to move your arms, and if you start your motion with your arms at waist height instead of lower and end it with your arms at shoulder height, you will change the angle and send the ball up instead of forward toward the net. Then your follow-through directs it to the setter.

The knee is on the floor to create more space between the passer and the ball. Arms are parallel to the floor so the ball goes straight up instead of forward.

Here's another position for passing close to the net. The center of gravity is low and elbows bend slightly. Just before contact, arms go into a scooping "J" motion that takes the ball up and away from the net.

A "J stroke" is sometimes used to pass when the ball is close to the net. Because of the J-like scooping motion of the arms, there's a back spin on the ball which pulls it back instead of pushing it forward.

Passing Zones

Here's a diagram of the passing zones for three people on the court. Notice the arcs drawn around the player on the left, on the right and in the middle. If you are on the right, you should be concerned with balls that fall within that space and to your right, but never to your left. The same goes for the left – never 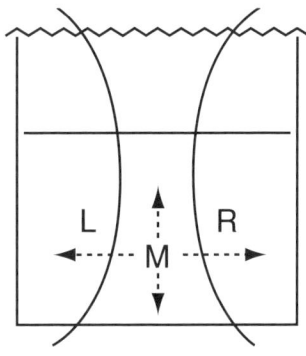 move to the right. The middle, however, moves forward and back but never to the line unless it is an easy serve and you are freeing the hitters to prepare to attack. The other situation that allows the middle to move to the line is when the ball is over the head of the passer on the left or right.

When you're on the right and moving to the right, your right foot moves first. Your move should include a little side skip, so make sure your right leg stays in front of your body. This will help control the direction of the ball. If you must move more than a step and a skip, your right foot moves first and your left foot crosses in front, never in back. During the crossover, make sure your face and shoulders are facing the oncoming ball. After the crossover, make a side hop. If you are on the left side, the left leg goes to the front, then you reverse everything and end with a left-right hop, especially if you're moving forward in the left zone. If you are in the middle, you still want the ball to go a little to the right, toward the setter, so you should have your left foot forward.

- **Moving to the right: right foot first, left leg in front, skip/hop.**
- **Moving to the left: left foot first, right leg in front, skip/hop.**
- **Remember: Always cross your legs in front.**

Most of the time, you shouldn't have to move more than what I've just described. If you need more than two steps, you should run as fast as possible, gradually lowering your center of gravity as you get closer to the ball.

On a deep serve, your job is to cut the ball off before it gets to the back line or the corners of the court. To do this, avoid backing up to pass while the ball is on its way over the net. Use an overhead pass if it's a slow ball or a lateral push from the side to cut the path of the ball.

Even though you might not be passing the ball, you should still move toward it and behind the other passers because 1) if you're there early enough, you can call the ball and 2) if there's a deflection or bad pass, you're already in motion to chase down the ball.

Note: The middle-back passer always moves behind the right- and left-side passers on a high ball even if these passers are actually passing the ball. This is called "butterfly passing."

Drills

You should always learn to pass with the ball coming over the net, so make sure to incorporate the net in whatever passing drill you are doing. Also, you'll need to develop good balance and increase your lower body strength to be a great passer. Free weights, squats, jumping jacks and lunges are all good exercises for passing.

Stationary Shuffle Drill

Time each other to see how fast you can get into the passing position by shuffling across the back court until someone blows a whistle. Then everyone moves into the passing position. Do this from side to side and front to back.

Bench Passing Drill

Sit on a bench with your feet and hands in the passing position and have a partner toss a ball to you. Then pass the ball back to your partner as she moves to different spots in front of you.

Between the Legs Drill

On the court, have one person toss the ball over the net in your general direction, and move across the court so that the ball passes through the space between your open legs. This teaches you to line up with the ball.

Belly Button Drill

Catch the ball near your belly button, in a low passing position. Your partner may throw the ball anywhere, and you should get to the ball in the correct position.

Passing Catch Drill

Have your partner pass the ball over the net to the back court and pass it forward toward the 10-foot line. You must run and catch it before it hits the floor. Make sure you're catching the ball in front of the 10-foot line and not too close to the net.

6 Hitting: Respect Your Height

There is no bigger crowd-pleaser in volleyball than the spike and kill from the hitters. In its perfect form, the setter sends a high ball across the court to the outside hitter, who is waiting behind the lines, almost lurking in the shadows. As the OH sees the ball coming, she starts her approach and with a high-flying jump smacks the ball into the other court, where it hits the floor with the sound of success. Celebration erupts in the gym as the score changes and the players regroup, congratulating each other as they go.

People think you need to be tall to hit a spike, but it's how you use what you've got that makes you a star. If you have the height, by all means, use it to swing your arms down and drive the ball downward into the opponent's court. But if you're not that tall, you need to respect your height, increase your strength, and develop the ability and agility to make contact with the ball at its peak. Shorter girls need to increase their speed on their approach to propel them higher into the air, and extend their arms and body into the ball. Then they finish with a snap of the wrist instead of a swing of the arm. This will send the ball hard and deep into your opponent's court.

Most hitters think they need to drive a spike straight down, but if you can fiercely hit a ball across the court, the chances of your opponent digging that ball are slim. Sending the ball hard and deep in the opponent's court actually increases your odds for a kill. You have less chance of being blocked at the net and a greater chance of your opponent missing the dig. If you tentatively hit the ball, regardless of your height, odds are that the ball will remain in play. And sometimes just keeping the ball in play is the smart move, especially if the set is bad.

All players should aim for a hard and deep hit into the opponent's court by making contact with the ball at its highest point with little or no follow-through. Shorter girls need to do this every time. Taller girls have a few choices. Because they have more height, taller girls can choose to hit the ball at a lower height (which may be a shorter girl's maximum height) or to follow through and drive the ball straight down. The bottom line is that the ball needs to clear the net, and because taller girls have more room to do that, they have the advantage.

If you are shorter, you need to make sure all your sets are off the net. You should hit the ball when it is at least 12 inches away from the net, and your setter should know this. If she sets the ball three to four inches away from the net or near the top of the net, chances are you won't clear it. When the ball is away from the net, you can see your blockers, have more options, and can pick your shots.

Technically, a spike starts with an approach toward the ball, not the net. Wherever the ball is set, if you use specific footwork to reach the ball, steps that develop into a jump with a swing of the arm and snap of the wrist that sends the ball over the net, you are executing a spike.

When you first learn to hit, start from the back court and then work closer to the net. This is different from learning to serve, where you start close to the net and then move back.

Breaking Down the Spike

There are several parts that combine to make a perfect spike, including the approach, the footwork, the swing, the jump and the follow-through. There are also several things you should know if you are spiking from the outside, middle, right side or back court.

On the first step of your approach, your hands cross in front of you, at waist height, and then go all the way into the back swing, as far as they can go. On the take-off, they come from the back and go straight up in front of you. As you jump your head is up and your arms move into position. Your non-hitting arm extends in the direction of the ball and your hitting arm goes back in a "bow and arrow" motion, with the hitting arm pulling back on the imaginary bow. If you're a lefty, do this in reverse. At this point, you want your shoulders and chest open as much as possible and away from the ball. This gives you maximum rotation for contacting the ball. And then you hit!

Bow-and-arrow position

Arms and Hands

Before you make contact with the ball, the upper part of your hitting arm is parallel to the floor, and your hand is behind your ear with your palm facing up. As soon as your hitting arm comes through to make contact with the ball, your non-hitting hand comes down and into your body. Contact is made with a wide-open hand and relaxed wrist, so that your hand rolls over the ball freely. On contact, shoulders and elbows lock and there's a quick snap of the wrist, and if you contact the ball high enough, you'll follow through with your entire arm.

Your arms play a huge role in the approach to a spike, especially before you start your approach. Your arms, with your elbows bent, should be close to your body as you start to run, slide or side-step to the spot where you're going to start your approach. Your arms never swing back and forth as you approach the ball because it interferes with your natural rhythm.

Arm motion for the spike

The Feet

To learn how your feet should approach the spike, start with the finished position and work backward because the last two steps are the most difficult to get. The last two steps are the take-off phase. During this phase, your feet should be pointing in, slightly pigeon-toed. Pointing your toes in helps your body rotate naturally after take-off. This rotation also helps confuse your blockers because they can't tell where and when you'll hit the ball.

The first step in the take-off phase is called the breaking step because it breaks your momentum and allows you to plant your feet after the hop into the take-off. The breaking step with your right foot is normally the longest step or hop in the approach. After your breaking step, the left foot comes around to create the pigeon-toed position, and contact to the floor is made with a heel-to-toe rotation to the outer portion of your shoes. This gives you stability and balance before the final take-off. If you land flat-footed or

Footwork for the spike approach, first step with left foot.

Left foot or second phase, body goes into flight.

Right heel plants on the floor to create the breaking phase.

Left leg comes around to finish. Reverse this if you are left-handed.

on your toes, you won't get your maximum height, you might fall into the net, and worse, you may hurt your knees. Reverse the foot if you're left handed.

*Front view of the pigeon-toed posi-
tion, final phase before take-off*

*Notice how the heel stops the
forward motion. This is also known
as the breaking phase.*

On take-off, your left foot is slightly in front of your right
(if you're right handed, it's the reverse), and your weight is
evenly distributed on your feet. Your knees are bent and
almost touching, your body and shoulders are leaning forward and your arms are in the back-swing phase. You've
landed on the ball of your left foot with your heel barely
touching. You are compressed like a spring ready to ex-
plode. And then you jump!

**Practice the jump: Stand on your left foot (if you
are left handed, stand on your right foot) and practice the slight hop into the take-off position. It is a
quick right-left (reverse if you're left handed),
where the left foot comes around and sticks to the
floor. When you have mastered this, you can add
the two or three steps to get to this point.**

Three-step drill for take-off, working backward:

1. From the take-off phase, and with a tennis ball in your hitting hand, take a step with your right foot and bring your left foot around, creating a pigeon-toed position. Jump and throw the ball in a spiking motion over the net to a teammate.

2. Working backward, stand on your left foot (lefties do the opposite), push off from that foot into the right-left pigeon toe or jumping phase of the approach, and throw the tennis ball over the net to your teammate.

3. Then take a step back, stand on your right foot (left for lefties) and go into the left, right-left jump. Throw the tennis ball over the net.

Throughout this drill, with all the motions, have the vision of hitting in your head. Then switch sides with your partner.

The Jump

When you jump, your body quickly goes through five different motions: a forward running motion, a take-off and a jumping motion, a hitting motion, a landing motion and a recovery motion. You're contracting and releasing hundreds of muscles through all the actions, so it makes sense that stronger elasticity makes one person a better jumper than another.

The heel stops the forward and starts the upward motion. And as in the song, "the heel bone is connected to the ankle bone," your calf is the next muscle called into action. By planting your heel, you're extending your calf muscle, getting it ready for contraction. If you land on your toes, your calf muscle is shortened which means you won't get the maximum push out of it.

> **In the jump, your heel is the key, as you are redirecting your forward motion into an upward motion.**

After your calf muscles come the quadriceps, hamstrings and gluteus muscles. Because your knees are bent, the quads and gluts go into their contracting and releasing motions. Then the back muscles pull the body backward and cause the abdominal muscles to extend and prepare to contract as your shoulders and arms take over. This is before the release that creates the whip-like motion of the body into the ball, sending it, with all your power, into the other court. And then you land with your knees bent and hands ready to block, dig or pass the ball if it is still in play.

The Head

During the approach, your head stays up the entire time. On contact, your head goes down in a whipping motion. If you wear your hair in a pony tail, it should flip up. If not, you're not using everything you've got to hit the ball.

> **Practice the jump without hitting the ball. With the proper approach and take-off, jump freely and feel how the body moves through all its motions. Then have someone toss the ball to you and catch it at its highest point as you jump. Then hit the ball instead of catching it.**

For Shorter Hitters

The speed phase, before the approach, includes more steps for shorter players. Taller and stronger girls usually use a short left, long right-left jump (reverse for lefties), but shorter girls should try a four-step run with a right, left, right-left jump. These extra steps increase your speed and give you more power in your jump which will propel you higher.

The "C" Positions

While you may look like you're lurking in the corner, as the outside hitter, you have your body in a forward position during the approach to a spike, with your shoulders and head out in front of your feet. And like a chain where each link pulls it weight in sequence, every part of the body works in sequence in the spike.

Before take-off, your knees are bent (not past 90 degrees) and your body comes from the forward leaning position, through the upward jump position, and into the "backward C" position. Think of your entire body curling up into a ") " position, with your knees bent, back arched and arms up and back over your head. If you do yoga, it's close to the half bow position. The backward "C" creates tension in your stomach during flight, whipping you forward and giving you the extra power to hit from your body. Then, as you make contact with the ball, your body reverses into a "forward C."

The backward "C" from two angles

The Recovery After the Spike

Let's hope you're high-fiving your teammates because you have scored the kill, but if the ball is still in play, you need to get back to a defensive mode.

Never stop playing until the ref's whistle blows!

When you land, make sure your body weight is not pushing you forward into the net. Even though your spike is executed perfectly with all the necessary fundamentals, if you touch the net or go under it and the ball is still in play, your opponent gets the point. Be sure to bend your knees when you land and, if necessary, take a small step forward or to the side.

The Approach for the Outside Hitter

The outside hitter approaches at an angle because it gives her a greater portion of the court to hit. Many girls in high school overhit the spike, so aiming diagonally across the court has the largest target. But all hitters should learn to hit straight down the left line, to the hole in the middle or across to the far corner. Being able to hit to all three parts of the court should be one of your goals as a hitter, along with learning to face the right side of the court and hit across your body to the left side of the court.

Here is the approach for the outside hitter. The first picture is the ready phase. The next picture shows the first step with the left foot. The third picture is a quick right-left with the feet and a back arm swing. In the final picture, the body goes into flight at the ball.

The Approach for Right-Side Hitters

The approach from the right side changes because of the hitter's more dominant hand. In theory, a left-handed hitter on the right side is the same as a right-handed hitter on the left side, and a strong left-handed hitter playing right side is a coach's dream. But often, right-side hitters (or opposite hitters) are right handed. Because of this, you need to start inside the court with a short right step that faces the body slightly to the inside of the court and the shoulders toward the net. The left foot comes around and steps left, followed by the right-left jump. If the right-side hitter is left handed, then the approach is the same as for a right-handed hitter from the outside.

The Approach for Middle Players

A middle player's primary roll is to block and freeze the blockers so the other hitters can have a one on one with their opponent's blockers. As a middle player, you shouldn't be upset if you don't get many sets in a game as hitting is not your primary roll, unless there is a mismatch in the middle (and that's the coach's plan for that particular match). When called to hit, most middle hitter/blockers use a quick or short left and then a right-left jump (depending on the dominant hitting arm). Because this play is so quick, you don't have time to take as big an approach as outside hitters do. As a middle, you need to make yourself available at all times for the setter, especially if it's a bad pass, because the blocker won't expect a set to the middle.

As the middle hitter moves away from the block and the net, you should be ready to hit. At some point, as you back off the net, the ball has to pass you on its way to the setter. Imagine a line from you that intersects the path of the ball. That is your point of reference. Start your approach as soon as the ball passes that imaginary line through your body on its way from passer to setter. But note, too, the height of the ball. If the pass is high, you might come in too early and if the pass is low, you might be too late, so use that imagi-

Approach for right-side hitter: Start with right leg in front (right-handed hitter) and inside the court. Left-handed hitters do the opposite. Arms go forward with the left foot.

Feet come together and arms go back for back swing. Body goes into flight. Left hand goes up, right hand goes back.

Body starts to create the backward "C," and is ready to hit in full backward "C" position in the final photo.

nary line as a point to stop backing up and start your approach to hit a quick set.

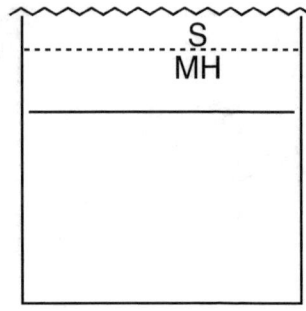

You never want to position yourself past the setter, meaning closer to the net than the setter, before you jump. You want to position yourself so that you take off an arm's length away from the setter and the ball. The ball should never come over your head after the pass, and you should never turn your back on

Picture an imaginary line between the MH and the setter that the MH never crosses.

the passer. Always open your body toward the passer, turning right or left depending on the direction the ball is traveling as you're backing off the net. If the ball does go over the middle of the court, whether it's a free ball or served ball, move to your stronger side for the approach and get ready to hit.

The middle starts the approach for a quick set as soon as the ball crosses the imaginary line I mentioned earlier. The height of the pass is also a factor to take into consideration for the approach. If it's a high pass, the approach is a little delayed and should begin as the ball starts its descent. If it's a quick or low pass, the middle's first step or approach starts right as the ball passes your imaginary line.

Hitting a Slide

Middle hitters should be able to hit a slide, as they are the ones called on most often for this play. A slide is a running approach behind the setter and a jump off the left leg to hit the ball before it gets to the antenna. There are actually three ways to run the slide:

1. The MH steps to the middle, faking a quick set while making sure that the right foot stops at the setter. She watches the ball leave the setter's hands, and then turns with left-right running steps and jumps off the next left

before hitting the ball. I think this is the best way to hit a slide.

2. This is a diagonal approach where the MH turns and runs after the ball, jumping off the left leg.

3. On this slide, the MH takes her approach along the 10-foot line and, at the last minute, turns in at the ball and jumps off one leg. This move is a little deceiving, but it can be read by the blockers.

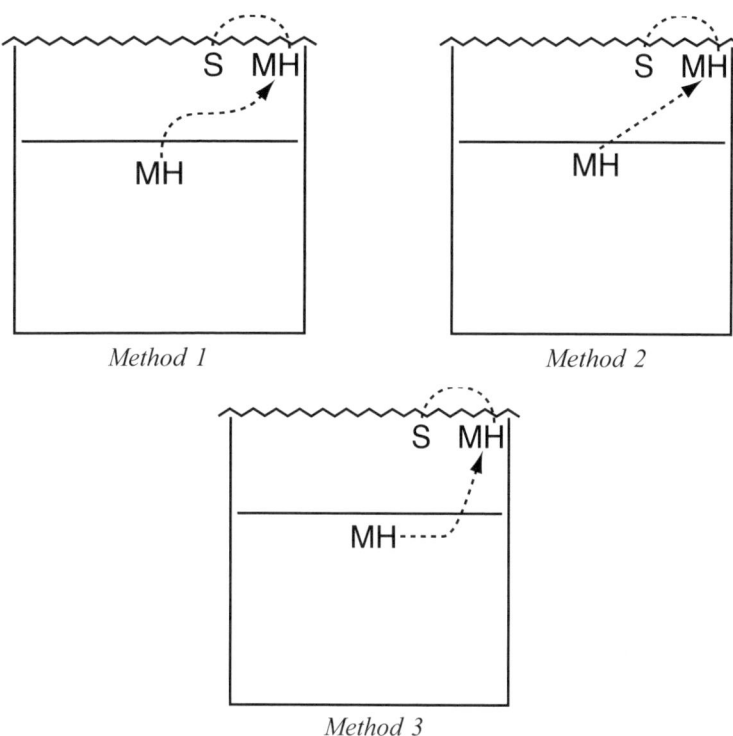

Method 1   Method 2

Method 3

Shorter middles have a lower center of gravity, which makes it easier to change direction on the approach. If you can change direction quickly, use it to confuse your opponents. Scramble around before you get to the setter for a quick hit. If the setter calls for a 1-Ball, fake a 31 and step back toward the setter for the set, or fake a Front One and hit a slide or a Back One.

If you're a taller MH or you have a very good vertical jump, you should take off before the setter releases the ball. If you are shorter, less strong or just don't jump high, take off after she releases the ball. Always open up your hitting shoulders to the setter and get your hitting arm up and ready to hit as soon as you take off. For every quick set, timing is the key, so make sure you spend time working on this with your coach and setters.

The Approach from the Back Court

In the back court, you hit the ball very much the same way as the outside hitter does. When hitting from the back court, however, you need to cover more ground before you make contact with the ball. To cover the extra ground, you need to use your hips more in the take-off phase by pushing them forward as you jump. By throwing your hips forward, you increase your speed and get to the ball faster without losing height.

Also, when hitting from the back court, there is very little follow-through because of the distance the ball needs to travel to get over the net. If you follow through, you may pull the ball down into the net or to the floor.

> **Remember: When hitting from the back court, you must take off from behind the 10-foot line. If the shadow of your foot is over the line, your opponent will get the point. After contact is made, you can land in the front court.**

The Tip

The tip, called the soft spike by some, is a very effective way to get a kill. The approach is the same as the spike, with your arms swinging up, but at the last moment, just before contact, you stop the swing and use your fingers for a soft touch or hard push on the ball. You should try to tip with a straight arm, with most of the motion coming from the wrist. If you tip with the palm of your hand or with the entire hand, the ref might call you for a lift. Before you tip, you should see the open space or hear your teammates or coach call, "Tip 1, " "Tip Middle" or "Tip 2." You need to listen and react immediately.

The right-hand tip: Notice how the arms start out like the spike.

Tipping drill: Practice tipping with your fingers, arm extended, with a soft touch on the ball. Then have someone call out where to tip.

Hitting the Ball Off the Blocker's Hands

Sometimes a hitter executes her hit with the goal of hitting the ball off the hands of the blockers on the other side of the net. But rather than blocking the ball back into the hitter's court, the ball goes flying off the blocker's hands, out of bounds, and the hitter scores a point. Sometimes this happens naturally, but a good hitter can make this happen, and a good blocker can't prevent it .

As a hitter, you might see the hands of the blockers just as you hit. If you do, you should aim for the outside hand of the blockers and use a swiping motion to direct the ball out of bounds. If the blocker jumps really high over the net, aim for her elbows rather than her hands. She'll have less chance of directing the ball into your court. Never aim for the palm of her hands unless the outside hand (the one closest to the antennae) is facing straight forward. The best time to go for an outside hand with an outside swing is in a tight set (close to the net), which will be blocked if you go for a kill.

Exercises and Drills

Plyometrics, where the muscle is expanded before it is contracted, will help your jumping skills.

Step-Up Drill

Place a sturdy box or step platform in front of you and step up and down on one leg 15-20 times. Then switch legs and step up and down again. Your knee should bend at a 90-degree angle on the box or step.

Box Jump Drill

With legs together, jump up and down on that same sturdy box 15-20 times.

Strengthening Drills

Work with a rubber band tied to a pole or to something sturdy behind you, and go through the arm motion of the hit. Crunches will strengthen your stomach muscles, which you definitely use in hitting.

Weights

Use light weights to press up from your shoulders for shoulder presses as described on page 39. Then, try one-arm rows: Bend over and balance one hand on a bench. Use a heavier weight in the other hand and pull that weight directly up to your chest. Extend that arm straight down to a few inches above the floor nd pull up again. Finally, switch to lighter weights for triceps kickbacks, where in the same position, you send your forearm backward as you straighten your elbow. Do these drills slowly, and do 15 should presses, 15 one-arm rows and 15 kickbacks as one "rotation." Do three rotations on each side.

Stretching

Stretch your arm across your chest, behind your head, over your head and straight back. If you're into yoga, try the Cobra and Upward Dog positions.

Blocking: The Soft Block and More

Most girls at the high school and club level can barely reach the top of the net. For them, blocking is not a big part of the game. Many girls comment that the difference between college and high school volleyball is the increased emphasis on blocking, especially since the move to rally scoring. But even if you can't reach the top of the net, there are still blocking options for you to learn while you are still in high school.

Blocking, which is executed at the net by front-court players, is the first line of defense. It stops an opponent's attack from coming over the net and sometimes forces a hitter to change her offense. There are three kinds of blocks, a stuff block, a regular block and a soft block, and there are different things you need to know as an outside blocker, right side blocker or middle blocker.

A *stuff block* forces the ball down on the opponent's side of the net with such force that there's no chance of recovery. You score the kill. A *regular block* stops the ball from coming over the net but often pushes the ball back into your opponent's court to remain in play. A *soft block*, which comes from the palms of your hands, slows down the ball as it comes over the net, and doesn't count as one of your three touches as long as you have jumped in your attempt to block. This block is used by those who don't have the height or ability to reach over the net.

Knowing when, how and where to block is the key to successful blocking. It's the same as knowing where to hang your hat so you can reach it — and not hanging it where you can't! If you can't reach over the net to stuff block a hitter, you should try a soft block so that the hitter will not continue hitting over you. And as with many other aspects of volleyball, timing is a very important factor in blocking. Jumping too early or too late will cause you to miss the block – and not reach that hat!

Blocking is one of the most difficult skills to execute in volleyball because every part of your body must work together. Where you focus your eyes, how you use your hands and shoulders, the position of your stomach, and where your feet go as you move across the court are all important in blocking. Remember, too, that blocking isn't always an individual activity; sometimes, you block as a team. Letting your teammates know the blocking assignments at the net without your opponents knowing is all part of your defense. Your teammates need to know what you are doing in the front so they can be in the correct position on defense in the back.

As a young volleyball player, you should make sure you know all these factors before you try to stuff or soft block someone. This takes playing with your head, at any height.

General Blocking Position

During the ready phase for blocking, your body weight should be distributed evenly on each leg, with your knees

slightly bent, shoulders in front of your toes, and hands in front of your shoulders with your fingers spread wide. If your knees aren't bent, you'll have to go down before you rise for the block, and you'll most likely be late for it. If your knees are bent, all you have to do is rise. Your hands are already halfway up and as you jump they go up and over the net toward the ball.

Ready position for blocking

During the block, make sure your hands don't touch the net.

The jump for the block starts with your legs coming up and out of the bended-knee position. As your body moves upward, your hands gradually slide over the net in the direction of the ball until your shoulders and elbows are locked, and you wait for the impact on the ball. It's as if you're waiting to grab the ball before the hitter makes contact – but don't do that! If you touch the ball on the other side of the net before the hitter does, she will score the point.

After take-off, your legs should be straight with a forward kick from the hips and the stomach tight and pulled in. Your shoulders are locked at the ear, and the arms are straight with your head up, and the eyes are fixed on the ball and the hitter's hand. The farther you can reach into your opponent's court during the block, the more effective you will be at blocking.

After contact is made on the palms of the hands, the wrists bend down into the opponent's court in a motion you'd use to play the piano, and then return up so you don't hit the net. Even if contact is not made with the ball, the entire procedure must be carried out with the correct timing because the back-court defender reacts to what takes place with the block.

The Soft Block

The ready position and jumping phase for the soft block is basically the same, except that your hands don't go over the net: you make contact with the ball on your side of the net. Your hands go straight up, with your wrists bent backwards for the

Position of hands for soft block

block, and you contact the ball with the palms of your hands. This causes the ball to go straight up on your side of the court.

A soft block doesn't count as a touch. After a soft block, be ready to hit the ball again or do whatever comes next.

Timing the Stuff Block

Timing is a major factor in blocking. You must time your jump so that you can change the direction of your hands, reach your hands over the net, and change the direction of the ball after contact is made. You must be able to take your hands back over the net before you lose height on your jump and your hands touch the net.

A blocker has less time in the air than a hitter, because the hitter is coming into the jump from an approach, but the blocker is jumping from her stationary position – also known as a dead jump. Consequently, the hitter has the advantage of height and momentum in the jump and you, as the blocker, must be very patient.

For you to be in your jump when the hitter is making contact with the ball, you must first see where the setter is sending the ball. Then you must take your eyes off the ball and look at the hitter whom you are blocking. If you don't see the hitter during take-off, your jump timing will be off and the ball will be in your court before you know it. Also, when you're ready to jump, make sure that your body lines up directly in front of the hitter's hitting arm, not in front of her body. By using your body to spot the hitter's hitting arm, it's much easier to eliminate the three major shots she has: the cross-court, to the middle and down the line.

Timing the Soft Block

With the soft block, you're contacting the ball just as it crosses the net. Therefore, **your jump starts with the hitter's swing.** Because contact is later, after the ball is over the net, you give the hitter time to jump before you jump. Then you must see the ball hit your hands so you will know when and where to direct the ball.

> **Because you usually don't have time to send the ball to a particular player, the emphasis of the soft block is to get the ball up in the air on your side of the court. This creates more time for someone else to get to the ball.**

Soft blockers attack the ball, but in an upward motion and on her side of the court. As a soft blocker, make sure that you are not too far off the net because you might get hit in the face or chest by the ball. You also don't want to be too close to the net either, because the ball will go over your hands. Also, if your hands are below the tape or top of the net, the ball will go over your head.

Timing for the Middle Blocker

The timing for the middle blocker is a little different regardless of whether it's a stuff block, regular block or soft block. The MB jumps with the hitter only because the ball is much lower and the hitter is much quicker. If you wait to jump, the ball will be on the floor while you are going up. If your timing is off on the middle jump, you should aim for a soft block because you will not have time to get over the net to make a block on the ball.

> **To be an effective middle blocker, you want to force the middle hitter to hit away from the line of approach. Her line of approach is the direction she is facing when she takes off, as that is her strongest hit.**

Keep Your Eyes Open

Don't close your eyes during the block. You'd be surprised how many players do, not only in high school but even at the elite level. You want your eyes to be wide open because you might have to change the direction of your hands during the hitter's flight. Some hitters are very smart, and if they see you blocking, they'll change the direction of their hit or even change to a tip. You need to see that.

Body Awareness During the Stuff Block

While your body is in motion during the block and your mind is fixed on blocking the hitter, you must concern yourself with the amount of space around you that you have to work with during the jump. The net is right in front of you, so you should always know the distance you are to it without physically looking at it. You also must be aware of the antennae, leaving only about 18 inches for the hitter to get through if you are blocking on the outside or right side.

Remember that defense starts with blocking, and although the players at the net are the ones doing the blocking, the players in the back court must know what area of the court you are protecting so they can fill in the open spaces. For the stuff blockers, although you are trying to block the ball, you are also protecting the larger area of your court at the same time, so know where your teammates are at all times.

Your Hands in Blocking

When you are blocking at the net, be aware of the position of your hands in relation to the side of the court you are blocking. If you are blocking on the right side of the court, you must make sure your right palm is facing into the court and the left palm is facing the ball. If you're blocking from the middle, both palms should be facing the ball. And if you're blocking from the left side, the left palm should be facing into the court and the right palm facing the ball. The ball should hit between the palm and the lower, meaty portion of the hands.

Hand position for blocking on the left-side of the net – start and finish

Hand position for blocking on the right side of the net – start and finish

Hands in position for blocking and finishing in the middle

> ## All hand motions from the block must finish down and in the direction of the larger portion of the court.

Finally, on a stuff block, whether you touch the ball or not, your hands must penetrate your opponent's court then pull back in order not to touch the net.

Landing

Everything that goes up comes down, so be sure when you land from your block that you always land on both feet. Occasionally a hitter ends up under the net, and if you come down on her foot, you can get hurt on your landing. If you see a hitter taking a flying leap toward the ball and you think she might come under the net, grab on to the net to protect yourself. It's better to lose a point than to sprain your ankle.

Most sprained ankles in volleyball come from blocking, so always remember to bend your knees as you land. Bending your knees will also help you fall to the floor if you do roll your ankles. Plus, with your knees bent, you will be prepared for the next block.

Double Blocking

Middle blockers move from side to side to help the outside blockers form a double block, so their footwork must be fast on both sides. They also need time to move to the outside to double block and then to get back to the middle. The footwork on both sides should be the same.

To get to either side faster, try a step, crossover step, then put your feet together and jump. During this movement, turn your body so that your waist, hips and legs face the direction you're moving, but keep your shoulders, hands and head facing the net with your eyes fixed on the hitter. While you're moving, you must remain in the ready phase for the jump, or you will have a seesaw effect that will mess up your timing.

Ready position for three blockers: Middle blocker moves to the left by moving left foot first. Body stays square to net. Right leg crosses over to the front. Shoulders and hands stay square to the net. Left leg finishes last step. Blockers form a double block. To block to the right, move the right leg first, followed by left leg crossing in front, with right leg finishing.

Whichever side you are moving to, that leg will move first, so if you are moving to your right the right leg moves first and the left crosses over in the front — never in the back. Then the right leg comes around and plants beside the other blocker who is standing there in the ready position waiting for your help. That right leg acts as the breaking leg that will stop your body from knocking over your teammate. Your left foot then comes beside the right foot before you jump.

Both blockers jump to form a double block that makes it more difficult for the hitter to hit around. The same sequence occurs on the left, except the left leg starts and finishes the motion. A side step can be used as well, but should never be used when you must cover large area. Side steps are used mainly by the outside blockers because they don't have much room to cover. Outside blockers sometimes start with a step in and then take a step out before bringing their feet together, or start out and step in to help with the middle. Middle blockers sometimes take a side step in either direction to block a ball that is not too far away but is going away from them.

The crossover step should be used for anything more than one step away.

Outside blockers should know the crossover steps, too, in case they try to help with the middle and then must make it back to the outside to block.

Team Blocking and Combination Drills

Team blocking starts with identifying the hitters in the front court on the opposing team and then assigning a blocker to cover each of them. The outside (left-side) blocker, who is usually the outside hitter, is normally assigned to the right-side hitter or setter on the other team. The middle blocker is normally assigned to the middle hitter. The right-side blocker, who is usually the setter or the RS hitter, is assigned to the outside hitter.

Team blocking combinations come from the middle blocker moving to the right or left and forming a double block on one hitter. Occasionally, all three players in the front row move to the right or left to form a triple block, especially if the set is that obvious. Here communication plays a vital role as well as fast footwork.

Communication

Blockers' communication is a must, especially in combination offense. For example: The right-side hitter you're assigned to block might hit in the middle and the middle hitter might hit on the right. There must be some verbal communication between the blockers indicating that switch. But you don't have to chase your hitter. The trick is to make sure your teammate knows of the switch and picks up the hitter that is coming to her.

Drills

Seated Chair Jumps

Sit on a chair in front of the net and assume a blocking position, with your arms and hands in front of your shoulders. From the sitting position, go straight up into a jump, land and sit back in the chair. If you can't go over the net, go straight up with a soft block.

Low Net Drill

Drop the height of the net to just below the height of the blockers' eyes. Have the blockers stand at the net with arms extended over it. Have the coach hit balls from behind the net to the hands of the blockers, and at the same time tell them where to rebound the balls — straight down, to the left or right. Then have a teammate stand on the other side of the net and *gently* throw the ball to the blocker's forehead. Instead of shutting or blinking her eyes, she should try to keep them open and see the ball as it makes contact with her forehead. This will help the blockers keep their eyes open during the block.

Pick-Up Combo Blocking Drill

This is a drill for three or more players, where they join the line at the net, block on the right and move across the net, blocking as they go. One of the goals of this drill is to increase verbal communication among team members and to practice their footwork as they travel across the court.

Start with three blockers at the net with (1) on the left, (2) in the middle and (3) on the right. All three jump at the same time in their respective positions. Then the blocker in the middle (2) moves to the right and forms a double block with the right- side blocker (3) and they jump together.

They then both move to the middle and jump, as a new person (4) takes the position as the right blocker and waits. The first right-side blocker (3), who has jumped two times already, then moves back to the right to form a double block with (4). They jump together and (2) moves to the left and forms double block with (1). After (2) and (1) jump, (1)

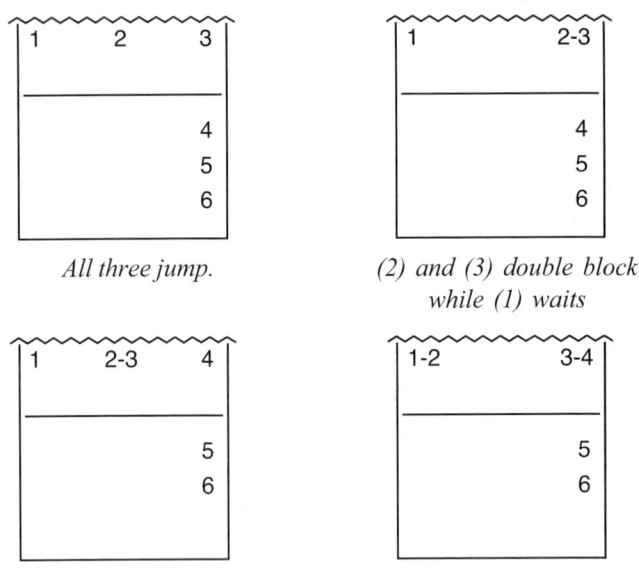

All three jump.

(2) and (3) double block while (1) waits

(2) and (3) form a double block in the middle while (4) waits.

(3) moves to form a double block with (4). (2) moves to form a double block with (1).

```
┌─────────────────────┐   ┌─────────────────────┐
│ 2     3-4      5     │   │ 2-3          4-5     │
│                     │   │                     │
│ ─────────────────── │   │ ─────────────────── │
│                     │   │                     │
│ 1            6      │   │              6      │
│                     │   │              1      │
│                     │   │                     │
└─────────────────────┘   └─────────────────────┘
```

(1) leaves. (2) stays and waits.   *(2) and (3) block and (4) and (5)*
(3) and (4) block in the middle.   *block. (2) leaves, (3) waits*
(5) waits.   *and (1) joins in line.*

joins the back of the line and (2) becomes the waiting outside blocker for (3). The process continues with (5) and (6) and so on, depending on the number of people you have. During this drill, players should be communicating as to where the next blocker should be going. Players should be calling,"Here," "Middle" or "Left."

Exercises for Blocking

Shoulder Presses

With light weight dumbbells (2-3 pounds) mimic the action of the block. Do three sets of 15.

Push-Ups

See volleyball push-ups in Chapter 2. Do three sets of 15.

Butt Lift

Lie on the floor with your knees bent and feet flat, about 10 inches apart. Then push up, lifting your butt in the air. Do three sets of 15. Repeat the same motion on one leg with a set of 15. These exercises will build your glutes, hamstrings, quads and lower back muscles, which all help with jumping.

Lateral Jumps

Standing next to the sideline with both feet together and knees slightly bent, jump over the line and land on both feet on the other side of the line. Do this for one minute. You do aobut 50 jumps in a minute. These jumps will build the lateral muscles you need for those lateral steps in blocking. Squats and side lunges will also help develop the muscles used in blocking.

8 Defense: Where Individuals Work as a Team

If offense is attacking the ball, defense is stopping that attack and launching your own. While there are many positions and plans for team defense, everyone on the team plays a role in defense at some point in the rotation and should know some individual defensive skills. Perfecting your defensive skills will earn you a spot on the team and win you the respect of your teammates and the crowd.

The primary goal of the defense is to keep the ball off the floor and in play. To do this you'll need to dig, but you may also need to roll, sprawl, collapse, pancake, poke or dive to reach the ball. Mainly, your job is just to keep the ball off the floor in the hopes that your setter or one of your other teammates can keep it in play and get it over the net. Sometimes, too, you may be able to thrill the crowd with a diving, rolling, last-ditch, point-saving effort.

Good defensive players need speed, quick reflexes and good ball control, and before you learn to do any one of the emergency plays, you must first learn to pass, as we discussed in Chapter 5. Most defensive plays come from the forearms, but any part of the body can be used to keep the ball off the floor. It's also important that you know which parts of your body should never touch the floor (injuries can ruin a game), and how to transfer the ball's energy into your recovery.

Finally, you need to know how your individual defensive skills work as part of the team defense.

Individual Skills

Digging is the most important skill in defense, and body control and balance are very important for digging. That's the reason shorter girls tend to be better defensive players. Since their center of gravity is lower, they tend to have better balance and find digging and playing closer to the floor a little easier. Usually they can get closer to the floor much faster than taller players.

A dig is essentially the same as a forearm pass, but because the speed of the ball is much faster, the angle of your forearm changes, depending on how hard the ball is driven. After the ball makes contact with your forearms, your elbows collapse or bend in a motion that absorbs the force of the ball. You don't push the ball to the target like I mentioned in passing, and there is no follow-through of the body after contact with the ball. The goal of the dig is to get the ball up and keep it in play.

Never dig a served ball. Pass it unless it is a very hard-driven jump serve and has the power of a hit. Digs come only from a ball that is attacked by your opponent. In the world of volleyball statistics, the number of digs you make will count toward a total for the game, tournament or season record books.

Although you may want to do a fancy, crowd-pleasing dive, roll, sprawl, collapse, poke or pancake, these are considered emergency plays and should be used only to survive an attack, when digging is not an option.

Stay on your feet and DIG!

The Dig

The dig is used for balls that are driven hard and hit directly at or in the vicinity of a player. While the goal is to get the ball up in the air, you are often limited by the height of the ceiling (if you're playing in a small gym), and also the speed of your setter. Don't concentrate too much on getting the ball to the setter, because the force of the ball coming at you will often send the ball over the net. Instead, try to dig it straight up. Obviously, if you can get it to the setter then do so, but sending the ball up high also gives her time to get it and your teammates time to transition from blocking to hitting.

Dig position

If you're not involved with blocking, get ready for the dig by keeping low. The ball on the attack is aimed at the floor and you are the difference between the dig and the kill. The lower you can keep your body and still be able to move quickly, the better. How and when you get low will determine whether or not you can move.

> **How do you know whether the dig is just okay or really good? When you dig the ball, if you can run and catch it before it hits the floor, it's a good dig.**

When you dig you can make a positive or negative mistake. Even though you want to get the ball to the setter, if you don't and it's high enough for the setter or someone else to play, it's a positive mistake. Another positive mistake occurs when you dig the ball and it goes over the net into the opponent's court and stays in play. When you dig the ball and it goes out of bounds, or you try to dig it and miss it completely, you've made two negative mistakes.

The ready position

The Ready Position

The ready position for defense is similar to the ready position for the forearm pass. Your feet are at shoulder's width, elbows are at your side, knees are bent slightly, and you harness your anticipation in a side-to-side motion. As the hitter is taking off, you move to a position where you are in a direct line with her, as if you are her target.

You must be able to see the hitter to be in a good defensive position.

The Dig Position

As the hitter makes contact, spread your feet and get as low as possible. At this point, your hands are locked in front and your body's center of gravity is forward, not falling back on your heel. Have your weight on the balls of your feet, with your shoulders in front of your knees and

The Dig Position: Hands go out toward the ball, and just as they make contact, they go into the body or pull back with the give and take of passing.

your knees in front of your toes. When you are in the correct stance, you would fall forward easily if someone pushed you from the back.

All movement must come to a stop when the hitter starts to swing at the ball. If you must move from point A to point B to dig, and the hitter is about to swing at the ball, you'll need to stop and get ready to dig. It doesn't matter where you are on the court. Stop and get ready to play defense. Sometimes you'll have time to hop into the dig position, but other times you won't.

When you make contact with your forearm, you should take or absorb the force of the ball, as we discussed in the chapter on passing, with a pull back of the arms or collapse on to your back. Remember, you will have better contact when you stay on your feet.

The One-Handed Dig

The one-handed dig is used on a hard-driven ball that goes off to the side. If it's on the left, the left hand goes out and meets the ball with a pushing motion. Contact the ball on the forearm, between the wrist and the elbow, as in an underarm pass. If the ball goes to the right, the right hand goes out, and on both sides the dig is finished with a slide on the floor or even a roll of the body over the shoul-

Ready position and one-handed dig: Step to the side and extend your body. Contact is made with the forearm.

Three very good drills for the one-handed dig:

1. Hit the ball off a wall with the forearm, alternating with your left and right arms.

2. Have a teammate toss very low balls to the side in a way that forces you to extend your body to dig it. Contact the ball with your forearm, with your thumb folded into the palm of your hand, your fingers straight and together and your wrist bent back. There is no follow-through with your hand. Just push the ball in an upward swing so that when it hits your hand, you fall to the side and recover by rolling over. Make sure you are back on your feet as soon as possible.

3. Bump the ball from one hand to the next while keeping hands locked or as above.

der of the hand that passes the ball. This is where ball control comes into play, as this skill should be used only in an emergency situation and not on balls that you could reach with both hands if you moved a little. Make sure you practice digging with one hand so you can develop the touch that is needed to execute this skill properly.

The Barrel Roll

Barrel rolls are used for balls hit to the side that you can only reach with full body extension. In the one-handed barrel roll to the right or left, your body extends, and your arms stretch out to the side and contact is made on the meaty portion of your forearms. Because your body is pulled off balance to the side, you want to land on the outer portion of your thigh and roll over on the same side you used to make contact with the ball. If you contact the ball with your right hand, the left hand is used to push the body up off the floor. If the ball is on the left, reach for it with your

Ready position for the barrel roll

Step to side and extend body. Contact ball with forearm.

Body extends on the floor after play. Note the right knee is turned in.

Left leg swings over the body, causing it to roll.

Left leg balances body while it and hands push the body off the floor.

Up and ready again.

left hand. Don't extend your right hand across your body as that will push your right shoulder forward and perhaps cause injury when you land on the floor. Also, make sure the back of your head clears the floor as you roll over your shoulder.

The Sprawl

The one-handed sprawl is used for slower balls and for those that are tipped over the blocker, while the two-handed sprawl is used for hard-driven balls. Both are used for balls that are hit two to three feet in front of where you'd nor-

Two-handed sprawl ready position   *Step forward to the ball with hands extended.*

Contact is made with both hands in front of the body.   *Body extends on the floor, ready to push up. Note: Body can go into a barrel roll or just stand up quickly.*

mally dig. With either sprawl, you end up on your stomach with your hand or hands stretched out in front so that the ball bounces high enough off your hand for a teammate to keep it in play.

With the one-handed sprawl, use the top portion of your wrist, as if you have made a fist and are scooping up the ball before it hits the floor. Most of the time, the hand that is not used to play the ball is placed on the ground during contact with the ball. The feet usually remain on the ground; however, one leg, more often than the other, will be off the ground so that the body appears to be in flight.

For the two-handed sprawl, dig the ball in a scooping or J-like motion while the body is falling forward. After the dig is made, you fall forward onto your stomach and use

---

Here's a drill for hitting the floor.

1. Stand at the back court line. Place the ball about 10 feet in front of you and have your partner stand behind the ball. Then take a few steps, drop one knee out to the side and extend your body to the ball, pick up the ball, toss it to your partner and hit the floor. No part of your body should touch the floor until after you pick up the ball and toss it. Do this a few times.

2. Next, have your partner move to the back court line with you. Walk up to the ball, bend over, pick it up, toss it up and over your head to your partner and drop to one knee like in step 1 and continue until you hit the floor.

3. For barrel rolls, go through the same motion for each phase. Do the same reaching, bending and tossing. Instead of sliding on your stomach after you toss the ball, roll to the right or left and get up as quickly as possible.

---

your hands to recover. The way the body finishes on the floor and the fact that a part of your body remains on the floor during contact with the ball is what makes the sprawl different from the dive.

How to Sprawl, Dive and Barrel Roll without Hurting Yourself

To learn how to hit the floor without hurting yourself, begin with Step 1 below, which starts closest to the floor. Then move on to Step 2, which lifts you off the floor a little before you try Step 3, which starts from the ready position.

1. Start with both knees on the floor in a kneeling position and go into an active sprawl, dive or roll, being careful not to hit your elbows or chin as you go forward to the floor.

2. Now raise one knee off the ground, kneel on the other and use your hands to walk yourself forward until you are spread out on the floor. The leg you push off with should end up straight on the floor and the other bent for the sprawl. Both legs must be straight for the dive, and start with hands first, then chest, and push with hands to create the slide. Hands may also be used for stopping the body if it's sliding too much. Hands should be used to push up off the floor as quickly as possible.

3. Next, start from the ready position for the dig and step forward with one foot, as if you are in slow motion, and go into the sprawl, keeping your elbows inside your knees and your knees bent. When you hit the floor, make sure you hit on the inside of your knee.

- For the dive, the body goes in flight, hands are first to hit the floor, then chest and then you slide.

- For the barrel roll, right hand goes up to the right, swinging in an upward motion, your body falls on the outside of your thighs and back of right shoulder, and your body continues in a rolling motion with the left hand coming over to push you back up.

Practice these three moves without the ball until you are comfortable with the motion and can do it without hurting yourself. Be sure to practice them on each side, to the left and the right.

Hitting the Floor

Knees should never touch the floor in defense. Kneepads are there to help prevent bruises and offer support for the knees, not to break your fall. Moreover, your elbows, shoulders, hips, toes, chin and obviously your head should not hit the floor during any of the skills. You take the force of the ball and transfer it into a roll or dive to minimize the amount of your body's weight landing on a particular joint. The point of these landings is to get yourself to the floor safely after you have lost your balance reaching for the ball.

Avoid sliding your hands, too, because you can get a burn from the floor. Try to dig the ball before it gets too close to the floor.

Most emergency plays finish with a roll, dive or slide.

The Collapse

The collapse creates more space between you and the ball when a hard-driven ball is very close to your body. Like it sounds, you collapse your entire body backward, falling away from the ball and landing on your butt. The momentum should carry you into a half backward roll so that your butt doesn't absorb the fall. Setters can use the collapse to set a very low ball, but it is most often used to the side, where you land on one cheek. As you reach to the side to dig the ball, keep your weight over the leg on the side where you're collapsing, and avoid hitting the floor with your elbows, wrists, knees or especially, the back of your head.

In the collapse, the center of gravity is lower.

Lean back to create more space between you and the ball.

Release the ball on the way down to the floor.

Collapse on back and spring forward.

The Poke

The poke is a high ball technique, used usually when your blocker has touched the ball, perhaps with a soft block, and the ball is traveling too high and fast to use an overhead pass. If you let it go, it will most likely go out of bounds, and you'll lose the point since it was your blocker who touched the ball before you. Here you want to make a fist and punch the ball up and toward your teammates.

The Dive

Here your body glides through the air on contact with the ball and you recover by sliding across the floor on your chest. Note that when you make contact with the ball, no part of your body is touching the floor. Contact is made with the forearm, whether it is with one hand or two. Only after the ball is played do you think about landing. The hands are the first part of the body to touch the floor, and they lead the body in a forward, pushing motion onto the chest. Then the body slides on the floor until it comes to a stop or until the hands stop it from sliding too far across the court. The dive is used mainly by men because of their additional upper body strength.

The Pancake

When you collapse or sprawl in time to scoop the ball up with the flat part of the back of your hand, as if it were a spatula flipping a pancake, you have performed a pancake. It's a skill that will usually surprise your opponents, but it's also one that is used as a last resort, when everything else fails – when the ball is so far away that a dive or sprawl will not reach it.

In the pancake, you slide your hand under the ball at the last minute, keeping your hand flat and the palm on the floor. Contact with the ball comes after the body slides on the floor. There is no upward motion of the hand so the ball doesn't get too high after contact is made. Go for a pancake only when the ball is falling in front of you. If it's falling to the side and you try a pancake, it will be difficult

155

Ready position for the pancake

Step toward the ball and drop to the floor.

Slide hand under the ball and pop it up.

Roll over on the same side as the extended arm.

Push off the floor.

Up and ready again

for your teammates to make the next play, unless someone runs in front of you before you make contact with the ball.

Most likely in a pancake, your body will be sliding on the floor to cover the extra ground needed to get under the ball. The nonplaying hand is on the floor as a braking device and is in line with the shoulders. Make sure your head is up so your chin stays off the floor and you are flat on your stomach so you don't burn your hipbone. The push-off leg should be straight and the nonpushing leg bent and out to the side. This position will allow you to get up more quickly. When you're training for the pancake, follow the same three training steps you used for the sprawl.

If you successfully make your pancake, be prepared – the crowd will be pleased with your effort, knowing that your hand is the only thing that separated the ball from the floor.

Defensive Zones

Before you dig, you need to be in position. Before you get into position, you need to know about the zones or bases. Defense starts with the block and then the back court players take over as they cover the open spaces on the court. Being in the defensive zone does not necessarily mean that is where you will be all the time. It means this is where the player needs to be before the hitter makes contact with the ball. This zone will change at times if there are holes in the blocks or if the blockers are not doing a great job at blocking.

There are two zones or bases for each player on the back court. Whether you choose to defend from first base or second base is determined by where the opposing setter sets the ball. Zone one or first base is for any quick set or tip from the setter. In this case, you stay where you are because you really don't have time to move. Use zone two or second base if the set is high to the front, back and back court. With these sets you have time to move to zone two or second base.

With zone one, the right and left back court players stand on the corner of the 10-foot line facing the middle player on the other side of the net. The middle back court player stands about four feet in the middle of the court from the back line. You should always establish the first-base position when your team is serving or if your opponent recovers your attack.

If the setter is setting the ball to the middle, zone one remains the same on the back court. No one moves; the only motion should be down and ready to dig the hit from the middle or the tip from the setter if she is in the front court. You stay there because the set is so quick you won't have time to move.

If the setter is setting the ball to the outside or left side, the back court players move to second base. If the ball is set to the left side, the right back court player drops back to the middle of the sideline and faces the hitter. The left back court player moves back on the sideline until her body is in line with the hitting arm of the hitter or the left shoulder of the middle blocker. The middle back defender drops back to the back line and lines up wherever the coach tells her to stand. Reverse the process if the ball is set to the right side.

The defense should not worry about any other positions or moves until they establish first and second base.

First and Second Base for Blockers

The first base for the blockers and back-court defenders is on the net with the right-side blockers standing at an

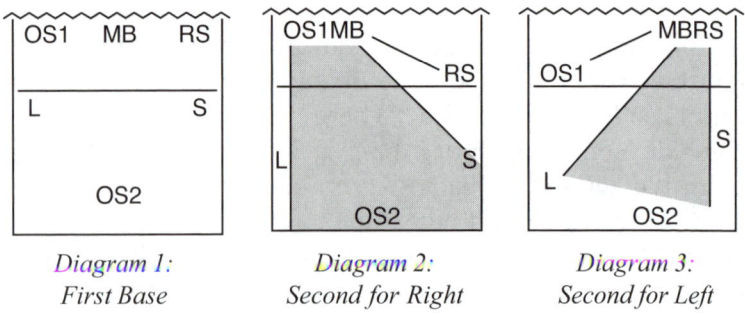

Diagram 1:
First Base

Diagram 2:
Second for Right

Diagram 3:
Second for Left

S = setter   MB= middle blocker/hitter   RS=right side hitter
OS1= outside hitter 1   OS2=outside hitter 2   L= libero

arm's length inside the court. The middle blocker is standing in the middle and the left-side blocker is doing the same as the right-side blocker (see Diagram 1). The libero is close to the left sideline and 10-foot line. The setter is close to the right side line and the 10-foot line. The outside is close to the middle of the court and in from the back-court line. All blockers are in their blocking stance. The second base for the middle blocker is to close the block to the left or right as she moves a few feet in either direction (see Diagrams 2 and 3). Also, second base for back court players changes, depending on which side of the net the blockers move to. If the ball is set to the opponent's outside hitter, the right-side blocker will jump with the middle to block, and the left-side blocker will drop off the net to the 10-foot line (see Diagram 3). Notice the change in defensive positon as back-court players move from base one to base two. The opposite will happen if the ball is set to your opponent's right-side hitter (see Diagram 2). If the ball is set to the middle, the middle jumps and blocks while the right- and left-side blockers turn and face the middle, getting as low as possible. That is the zone one defensive position for the right- and left-side blockers on a quick ball that is set to the middle where the middle is the only blocker. The back-court defenders stay in zone one.

9 Libero, Defensive and Serving Specialists: There is Room for You on the Bus

While some teams scrounge around to find six players, other teams turn away girls after they have accepted 16 or 18 players. However many you have on your team, there are three positions you should know about — libero, defensive specialist and serving specialist. While a specialist in any one of these positions may not play the entire game, playing these positions can hone your skills, put you in the game, and get you a seat on the bus.

Liberos, defensive specialists and serving specialists make the game more enjoyable to watch. In addition to the obvious advantages of having a really good passer or digger in the back row, or someone who can serve an ace in a pinch, having an L, DS or SS on the team gives more girls a chance to play and be part of the team. But the key to success as a specialist is to own the position, to be proud of knowing that you are the best passer on the team, a great digger or a dynamite server. Here, a patient and confident attitude counts!

If you are chosen as a specialist, make sure that you continue to work on your other skills. You don't want to stifle your overall progress by concentrating too much on one area. The goal of a specialist is to become a complete player.

The Libero

The position of libero – pronounced "LEE-bah-ro" or even "LEE-bro" – was added to women's college and club volleyball in April 2002. Most of the time, the libero comes into the game for the middle, who might not be as good at digging and passing balls from the back row as she is. Because the position is new, some coaches haven't added it to high school play. Hopefully that's not the case on your team, because a libero only adds to your team and takes away nothing.

Usually a smaller girl, the libero is identified by her opposite- or different-colored shirt and often looks like she is bouncing in and out of the game at will. But she is one of the most aggressive players in defense, showing no fear in hitting the floor, chasing a fly ball or crashing into the crowd just to keep the other team from scoring a point.

Because the position of libero is relatively new, here is a synopsis of the rules. For the official rules in their correct order, visit an official volleyball site, such as www.volleyball.org. But for an easier understanding of them, read on.

As an extra defensive specialist, the libero must wear a jersey of a color different than her teammates, must stay in the back row, and may not block but may serve in one rotation for each match. Coaches can choose the libero-as-server rotation at any time during the game. Each team may have only one libero among their 12 players and her number must be added to the score sheet before the match begins.

The libero can replace any player in a back-row position, and there is no limit to the number of times she can enter the game. There must, however, be a rally between two libero replacements, and the libero must be replaced by the same player for whom she came in. The replacements can happen only when the ball is out of play and before the ref blows the whistle. The libero enters the court by the sideline between the 10-foot line and the back-court line.

Here's the tricky part, or at least, the tricky language. The libero may not complete an attack-hit from anywhere, if at the moment of contact the ball is entirely higher than the top of the net. Essentially, this means that a libero can't hit like an outside or middle hitter if the ball is above the height of the net.

Taking this a step further, if a libero sends an overhead pass using her fingers or bump sets from a spot in the front zone, a front-court or back-court player may not complete an attack-hit on a ball and must send a freeball over the net. The ball may be attacked in the front zone if the libero makes the same set from behind the 10-foot line. For someone to attack the ball when the libero is in the front court, she must bump set the ball to the back court.

There are also special rules if the libero is injured and can't continue to play. She can be replaced only by a player who was not on the court at the time of the injury and can't re-enter the match. Her replacement must remain a libero for the rest of the match.

Defensive Specialist

A defensive specialist can enter the game for any one player and usually substitutes for any player in the back row except the setter. Where the libero wears a contrasting shirt, the DS wears the same uniform as everyone else on the team. The main difference between the two is that the DS can jump and hit from the back court, and she can go into the front court and set a ball while a teammate attacks it. Many teams have weak areas in defense and may utilize a defensive specialist and a libero at the same time. In high school, girls are often just starting out in volleyball and haven't mastered all the skills yet. One might excel in passing but not serving, or vice versa. At this level, a coach may need to take two or more players and turn them into one complete player until everyone's skills have developed.

Serving Specialist

Like a pinch hitter who is called in with the bases loaded and two outs, a serving specialist is often brought in and expected to rack up an ace or two at the most dramatic moment. For a serving specialist, accuracy and precision are crucial, as are consistency and the ability to remain calm.

A serving specialist must be ready at all times, be able to stay warm on the bench, come in for the big point, and hit a particular spot. The coach may signal where he wants her to put the ball, and she should be able to hit any of a dozen spots on the court. She should have a variety of serves in her pocket, and should also be able to dig and pass. Sometimes she will stay in that rotation, so she needs to know how to play defense in case the ball comes back to her.

Substitutes

Subbing gets more girls into the game, gives players a rest, allows the coach to talk to an individual player, and sometimes the coach to shake up the team a little.

A coach can substitute one player for another at any time, but those two players must play for each other for the rest of the game. In fact, the coach can even substitute a different player for the substitute as long as the third player hasn't been on the court yet, but then all three players are connected to each other for the rest of the game. Many coaches are unaware of this rule, so be sure to discuss it first. The number of substitutions allowed during a match in women's play is a total of 15 subs per team per game.

Beware, however, if you are called in to sub. "Hit to the new girl," is a phrase that's not only said on the other side, but listened to as well. When you come in, expect the ball to come your way. Always stay loose and be aware of what is happening in the game. If you don't, you'll be lost when you get in the game.

Training

These special positions can be very nerve-racking for the player in them, so create a training environment to simulate a lot of stress and then practice serving or digging. Get to the gym early, warm up and practice some serves and other skills before practice. Leave later than everyone else and practice some more. If you go this extra mile and become a libero, defensive specialist, serving specialist or sub that the coach can depend on, you will see lots of playing time, pull off what's necessary when called upon, and be a star on a winning team.

10 Using What You've Got for Offensive Might

I started this book by telling you that you can rule on the court at any height. And this is true, but to win a place on the team, to win games and matches, to win championships, you must use everything you've got and really want to excel.

If you're not the tallest or strongest girl on the team, you need to become the fastest and the smartest. You must pay attention at all times, both at practice and in the games. You should take care of your body by working out and eating well, learn about offense and defense by watching college and professional games, and learn about volleyball. Then you will be able to read your opponents, which means you'll be able to predict what they'll do and be there to keep them from scoring a point. One of my mottos is, "It's not necessarily how tall you are, but how smart you play." Some people can jump higher than the net but they don't play with their heads. They miss opportunities. They misjudge situations. They overlook the obvious.

Working Together

Volleyball is one of the few sports where nearly everyone plays each spot on the court. Every individual player is linked, and for everyone to work together, each individual must do her job. That means the server must get the ball over the net or the whole team will lose a point. The same goes for the passer, the setter, the hitters, the blockers and the defenders. To score one point in volleyball, each player must be on the same page. That's the reason each person should perfect three individual skills – passing, setting and execution – to get a point. Only then can they form a whole team out of six individual players on the court.

If you have a weak player, you need to adjust for that. That's where coaches must step in and use substitutions, whether it's defensive specialists, liberos, serving specialists or even a hitting specialist. But it goes even further than this; you must also know your teammates' strengths and weaknesses. If you have a weak passer on your team and the other team sees this, you and your teammates will need to be in motion when the ball is hit so that you can cover for her. If you have an exceptionally strong player on whom you can depend, you can also count on the fact that your opponent knows she's your strongest player and will work to diminish her effectiveness.

To be a winning team, everyone must contribute her own strength. Everyone must think as one team and play as one. This takes teamwork and communication. You know you should call the ball and help the setter at times, but you can also lend your eyes to your teammates by telling them what you can see that they can't. For instance, on an attack, if the nonhitting players can see open space, they should call plays such as, "The line is open," "Tip cross court" and "Push deep." And always call a "Free ball!"

When the Offense Starts

At the start of every point, the receiving team is considered the offensive team and the serving team is the defensive team. The receiving or offensive team is setting up the attack. Once the ball goes over the net after an attack that doesn't result in a point, the other team becomes the offensive team.

We covered many offensive plays in the chapter on setting. Take a minute to review them and then return to this page for more. We discussed the High Ball Outside, the

---

A good offense starts with a good pass.

Front One to the Middle, the Back One, the Shoot Set to the Outside, the Short Shoot or 31 Set, the Back Three or Four, the Back Court A-B-C, the X, the Split Set, the Slide Set and the Setter's Tip. These are some of the most common offensive plays. A team can use them to win any game, but what is important to learn is how, when and where you use them. It doesn't really matter how many plays you have in your playbook. It's how and when you use them, and where you choose to set the ball that will make the difference in the effectiveness of your offense.

Using Your Offensive Plays

To win games, you have to play smart, know the game and have a strategy. The first step in developing your offense comes with assessing the other team, and it only takes a few rotations to find their strengths and weaknesses. This girl is a power hitter. That girl has a weak serve. This girl always hits from the outside. The setter can't seem to back set. Things like that are obvious strengths and weaknesses that you will see right away. Within the first few rotations of the first game, you should pick out the player to target and the one to stay away from. Here your coach plays an important role in helping the team face a specific opponent, and he or she should have a plan in place to win the game.

After a few rotations in the game, the coach should know how to set up the plays that he or she wants the setter to run. The coach and the setter must also know when to call certain plays. For instance, if the game is very close, you never want to call a play that is difficult to run, or one you haven't mastered in practice. It's also important to spot your opening and set the ball there regardless of the play that you have called prior to the serve. This comes with experience, but it's important to start thinking about early on. As a setter, you always want to set the ball to your best hitter. But sometimes it's more important to match up your hitters against your opponent's worst blockers, and on combination plays, you want to set the ball to the attackers with one or no blockers.

> Set the ball where your attackers have a greater chance of scoring a point, rather than where your opponents have a better chance of blocking it.

Offensive Actions

Most teams in high school may have one outstanding player. She is the power player who serves consistently, blocks often, hits powerfully, passes directly, sets accurately and is there when you need her most. This is the go-to girl in most games. But in practice, the coach should focus on all the girls and all the skills, and develop offensive plays that will guarantee points for everyone. Combination plays are a good way to include more players in the offensive action.

For example, the X play requires the use of two front-court players. This play is called the X because the middle player runs to the setter and jumps for a one-set, then the right side player crosses behind the middle and hits a two-set next to the middle's left shoulder. The X happens as the two players cross each other. Most teams use the middle and the right side player for the X, especially if the setter is in the back court. This gives the setter the option to set the ball outside if the pass is not there to run the play.

In a play like this, and in nearly every combination play that I mentioned in the setter's chapter, you can use your best player as a decoy and set to someone else on the team to further confuse and surprise your opponent.

In the Game

While it's the coach's responsibility to develop a strategic offense, it helps the players to understand the strategies, so I have included here a few ideas for you to think about.

Run your offense with very few changes, unless your opponent is preventing you from scoring points. Then determine whether it is your offense that really needs adjusting. Don't abandon a good offense until you are certain it is the problem, and then be flexible enough to try something new.

One way to outsmart your opponent is by giving your second-best hitter the first few sets. Then run a combination play with your best hitter to get her going. Or do the opposite and give your best hitter the sets from the first ball and drive some fear into your opponent. This will help set the stage for how the rest of the game will be played.

Sometimes if your offense just isn't working well, it helps to put in a few different players. It changes the energy and throws off the defense, and sometimes causes your opponent to then change their offense. Don't, however, let the other team change your style of play. Some teams will try to do just that in order to break you. If for some reason your team begins to break down, the best way to get back on top is with a combination play that will guarantee a kill and get the spirit back in everyone.

A Word About Attitude

To win in volleyball, you must play smart, but you must also want the win. Some say it doesn't matter who wins, it's how you play that is important, but think about how you feel when you win and how you feel when you lose. To win, you must move beyond a player and become a competitor, a fighter, someone who rises to the challenges and takes pride in the game, win or lose. But remember that your coach always wants a win, even if it's an ugly win.

Leaders develop on every team, and you, too, can learn to pull your team together before, during and after every game, especially if you have the right attitude.

To Win at Volleyball

To win, you must keep your competitive edge and not give in to sentimentality. I had one high school team for four years, so some of the girls were graduating. This team had won the state championships for three years in a row and was ranked first in their league going into their final championship match. But before the big game they lost their edge. They cried after their last game in the regular season. They cried after their last practice. They cried after they won the semifinal. Then they cried *before* the finals. I couldn't believe it when they came out of the locker room, moments before the final match, weepy because this was their last game together. And you know what? They lost. They lost not because the other team was better. They lost because they brought their sentimental emotions onto the court. This day opened my eyes to another aspect in sports that coaches and teammates must deal with and prepare for. There will always be a last game as a team, because players in high school, club and college will always graduate and move on. Honor your time together, and don't mourn your time apart.

11 What Coaches Should Know

Just as volleyball players are always learning new things, so are coaches. Or at least they should be. Coaches have a special job that includes learning as well as teaching and coaching. These are three separate skills, and at practice, coaches teach, in a game they coach, and every day they learn.

The New Coach on the Block

When coaches join a team that has been together while, they must always remember that there was a coach there before them, and that the girls on the team may have strong feelings – good, bad or indifferent – for the previous coach. A mistake new coaches often make is saying something like, "Forget all that you learned before and play my way." Nothing will alienate the team from a new coach more quickly. Some girls may have an attachment to their prior coach and will take personally any negative statements about that coach.

Good coaches learn from their teams, and to do this, they need to find ways to get into their team's environment, to see who the team's leaders are and how the team works together. Coaches should take the time to meet each player and start to build trust between them. After this trust is developed, coaches can start teaching, but they must be careful to teach gradually.

If you, as the new coach, have a different coaching and teaching style than the previous coach, show the team how you do things and ask them to try it your way. Assure them that the end result will be the same. If they can't seem to let go of old habits or don't want to, tell them to practice your way as well as the way they know. The point to remember is this: If it's not broken, don't fix it, but find a way to make it better.

> Remember: You are there to make them better volleyball players. You are not there to change them.

The First Day

Coaches should always be prepared, especially on the first day, for lots of questions from the players. If the parents are there, meet with them first and go over the rules, telling them what is expected of them and what is expected of the girls. Then ask them to stick around for a while as you speak to the athletes.

When you first meet the athletes, tell them a little about yourself and share your major accomplishments and achievements. You want to create an environment in which the girls can't wait to learn from you. When you get to the rules, make sure the first few come from the former coach's rule book and then add your own as you go along. Keep the rules and the first meeting short and to the point, and end with questions and answers.

> Remember: Once you make the rules, stick to them. If you don't, you will lose the respect of your team.

Boundaries for Coaches

As the season progresses, coaches need to set up boundaries between themselves and their girls. These boundaries are not discussed or written down, but you, as the coach, need to be very clear about them in your own mind. Your players need to know when it is time to play around and when it is time to compete. Practices should be business

The Boundaries On and Off the Court

Here are five boundaries that I set and the appropriate behavior within each.

NEVER

No private social encounters, touching, hanging out , etc.

During the Game

Games are pressurized "business" situations. Girls should know this and should not bring any problems to the coach during a game. Coaches should never spend game time on one girl's performance, mistakes, problems or attitude. During a game, a coach is there to help the team win by observing both teams' offense and defense and instructing the team on how best to crush the other team's strengths and to exploit their weaknesses.

At Practice

Girls can approach the coach before and after practice about volley-ball-related issues such as private instruction, rules clarification, conflicts with other players, and explanations of why they are play-ing or not playing a specific position. If issues pertain to practices, they should be raised before the practice. If the solution or explana-tion is lengthy, the coach should set a time after practice to give a satisfactory answer. Some problems may need individual atten-tion, and coaches should deal with them at the end of practice or off to the side while other players are still around, and not behind closed doors.

In the Hallway

Girls can approach the coach about their problems before and after games, in the hallway, by phone or email. Some problems may be related to family, school, or physical and social issues. The coach should listen attentively, and offer to think through the problem and get back to the girl promptly, unless there is an obvious, simple solution. The coach should remember that he or she is not the par-ent.

At Home

Girls should never enter the coach's personal life (relationship, health, financial, physical, emotional issues), and the coach should never step out, meaning the coach shouldn't offer information or answer personal questions.

and after-practice time should be social. You can joke with them before and after practice, but during practice you are the teacher.

You, as the coach, must also determine how far the girls can take the socialization factor, because you should not tolerate wrongdoing on or off the court. Joke with them and speak to them as often as you can, but make sure the jokes stop as soon as it is time for practice or a game. You must always be in control of their respect, so if someone says something that is not appropriate, deal with it right away and then move on. You will gain nothing by letting a problem, issue or resentment fester within you or within your girls.

Get to Know Your Team

Knowing when to stick around and when to leave the team alone is tricky but important. Remember that distance is good but so is accessibility. Get to know your players' friends, their bus drivers, their teachers, and their parents. Take the time to learn about each player on your team and find out what makes her tick. Ask the girls questions about themselves. Find ways to encourage, inform and teach them. Get into their world as much as you can and let them into yours a little bit, but make sure you stick to your boundary line. If you are a male coach coaching girls or a female coach coaching boys, you must make a tighter boundary around yourself and make it very visible. Your team should know that they must show respect to you and your friends and family at all times, especially in public.

You should also learn more about coaching methods and styles from the many books on coaching volleyball, and look at books on coaching other sports, too. Attend volleyball clinics and seminars, speak to other coaches and share ideas.

The more you get to know your team, the more they will trust you.

Teaching Versus Coaching

Once coaches get past the drama that comes with coaching, they need to put their teaching skills into action. Hopefully your girls trust you, have confidence in you and are ready to learn. So now what?

Teach, don't coach!

Leave the coaching for games and to the professional coaches who spend most of their time working on plays. When you are in the gym with your girls, you are there to teach them the skills of volleyball and the elements of the game. Practice is all about your players learning from you, learning how to play the game and how to be a competitor.

After you teach them at practice and it is game time, you turn into the coach. As coach, you must sit or stand and figure out how to win the game. You're there to see what's working for your side of the court and what isn't. You're watching to see what is happening on the other side of the court and trying to find ways to counteract them. At this level, coaching is about what it takes to win the game, offensive and defensive strategies, your action and your opponent's counteraction.

Most girls and parents won't notice the difference between you as the coach and you as the teacher. In the public's eye, you will always be the coach. But make sure that YOU know the difference.

Coaching is about winning that day's game, about competition at the highest level, and about bringing out the best in your team.

Developing Your Coaching Style

When it comes to coaching, it doesn't really matter whether you were a good player or great player. Most coaches start as a player and have been coached by many people by the time they get their first coaching job. Regardless of the number of coaches you've had, one coach or style of coaching will influence how you coach and teach. But it is important to realize that no one style of coaching and teaching is right for every player. What might work well on girls might not work as well on boys. What might work well on 14-year-olds might not work as well on 18-year-olds. Even within the same team, what might work well on some girls might not on others. While some teams may respond to a harsh and strict approach to coaching, others will find it threatening and reject it.

As a coach you are dealing with many kinds of players – players of different heights, weights, body types, athletic abilities, races, ages and genders. This means you have to be flexible, understanding, tolerant and willing to learn from your players. You cannot have one style and expect everyone to learn from it. You will lose some of the kids along the way.

> ## A good coach needs more than one style of teaching.

Coaching High School Girls

When coaching girls, spend time with them on balance and coordination. They should learn how to manipulate their bodies in motion while rebounding a ball to the target. They should learn body control and how to avoid getting hurt when falling to the floor, as they are not as tough as boys. And they need to learn how to control their emotions when they let their teammates down. Girls can be very emotional and some cry easily.

One of the main reasons to have a variety of coaching styles is that you cannot coach high school girls the same way you coach boys, men or women. In high school, girls are just learning about their bodies. They are learning to deal with its changes, and some will be protective of themselves and shy away if the coach is a man. Boys will be a little more proud and open, and will accept a harsher style of coaching, although some girls will respond to that as well. By the time girls get to college and are called women, they have been through many stages and are stronger physically, psychologically and emotionally.

Never Embarrass Your Players

Intentionally embarrassing a player is one of the worst sins a coach can commit, and unfortunately it happens often. Whether you are at practice or in a game, and especially in a game, embarrassing an athlete can force her away from you and from the sport. If you have something to say to a player that might be embarrassing to her, take her aside or deal with it face to face after practice. If necessary, deal with it as a team. If something happens on the road, wait until you get home to deal with it, if possible.

Get Creative at Practice

Make practice fun but always keep it educational and competitive. If you do, the girls will enjoy themselves and get a better workout. Experiment with a player and an exercise, but make sure the exercise will make her a better player, and always tell the players how the exercise benefits them. Also, keep the girls moving at all times. That way, they won't have time to shelter or isolate themselves. If you see a girl shying away from the rest of the team, send one of her teammates over to aid her. In that way, she won't feel left out and it will build confidence and trust among the rest of the girls. If one gets upset or starts to cry, have a player who is respected by everyone console her.

It's difficult to know when to get involved and when not to. At times you have to be firm, and at times, soft. You have to make practice tough but you also need to be gentle with the emotions afterward. If you have a problem with an individual during practice, don't neglect the rest of the team to deal with it at the moment. In the future, the team may use this tactic to get out of practice and view you as a weak coach, one who can be manipulated.

Distractions

Outside distractions can cause a player to drift away from the team and from the game. As a coach, you must spot this problem, find out what it is, and deal with it as discreetly as possible. That means going to the source of the problem and dealing with it directly. Speak first to the player so that she has no surprises, and make sure she is comfortable with you speaking to the outside source. If it's a relationship problem with a boyfriend or friend, speak directly to that person causing the problem. Don't take sides, but let the person know that the problem is affecting the individual player and the team. Ask them to help make the situation better, not tell them what to do or what not to do, as that might cause some resentment. At all times, avoid confrontation. If the boyfriend or friend agrees to help make things better, that's great, but if not, then you must approach the player, let her know how you feel about the situation and tell her that she now has a choice to make. If she stays with the team, she'll need to leave her problem outside the door; if she can't, she'll have to leave the team. When she takes care of the situation, she can return but she will be on probation for a set amount of time. If school work is the problem, the player must stop practicing and playing until she catches up with her work, and then she can return to the team. But she will also be on probation for a specific time.

High school girls will use practice and games as excuse not to do their school work, so coaches must know how each girl is doing in her classes. Make time to speak to the teachers, deans and principals. It's a good idea to occasionally sit with the team and have a study session during practice. Encourage the girls to do their homework during their free periods instead of waiting until they get home, when they might be too tired. Learning to use their time wisely is a must if they want to play in college.

The Environment at Practice

When I speak about the environment in which we practice, I'm speaking about the tone, intensity, noise level and distractions around us. I work to create an environment that is as charged as the one in which we compete against another team. The energy of this competitive environment escalates when you compete on the road. To teach your players how to tune out all the distractions, I create the same situations at practice, especially a day or two before the game.

To create the environment, bring a CD of music to practice and turn it up. Use this distraction when you speak to them. Invite some friends to practice and have them cheer against your girls. Bring in a referee and have him or her rule unfairly against your girls so they can learn how to deal with bad calls. Make unusual substitutions and keep people on the bench to shake up the team. In short, make sure they know what to expect in a game environment before they get there.

At Practice

Once you've passed the stage of teaching the girls how to position their hands, how to approach the ball, and how to hit, serve, set, pass, and move on the court, you need to teach them how to play the game of volleyball. That, too, starts at practice.

After taking attendance, Begin each practice with warm-ups and stretches. Warm-ups can be any type of activity that boosts the heart rate and gets the muscles going. Jogging laps around the court is a good way to start and is what most coaches suggest. Then begin the stretches. Make sure the warm-up session doesn't occupy too much of the training session.

Ball control drills come next, and include bumping to yourself, single hand bumps, and passing back and forth to a partner. This set of drills ends with some peppering, where two players alternate with a bump, set and spike to each other. The coach can also hit or toss balls to the entire team, one player at a time, for a short period. Next comes an individual skills session, and that skill would then be incorporated into the entire practice. That gives the body of the practice session one goal, a goal that the coach reminds his players about throughout the entire session.

For example, if you are doing a wash drill, where your players must serve, pass, set, hit, block, defend and pass free balls coming from the coach, one of these skills should be the main focus. This doesn't mean that you should forget about the other skills, but that one skill must be emphasized at all times. For those unfamiliar with the wash drill, one team must score two or more balls in a row to get one point. When a team scores one, they immediately get another ball that they must score. If they don't score at that time, and the other team gets the point, then the drill is wash.

On the Bench

Make sure your players know who the starters will be and who will substitute for whom in a given situation. If a player is on the bench, tell her the reason she is on the bench. A player who sits on the bench should be fair to herself and the other players on the court. She must respect the fact that the other players have better skills and use that to challenge her personal best. If a player is upset that she is not starting or playing, remind her that the intensity she shows at practice and how she works with the team will convince you to put her in the game.

As the coach, you must never look like the bad guy for not playing a specific player. You need to know what a player will give you in a specific situation before you put her in, and you must see this in practice first. My mother used to say, "You must learn to dance at home before you can dance at the club."

Some coaches have favorites and this is very detrimental to your team's morale. Your girls will see this with the clarity of a Jamaican sunset, and their parents will go so far as to keep track of it in writing. If you pick favorites and continue to do so, you may find yourself looking for a new coaching job at some point.

If you have a player on the bench who sits a lot, and the parents always come to the game, approach the parents ahead of time and explain the reason their daughter sits. Do it before they come to you. Your reasons must be true, logical and clear. Then do your best to put all the athletes in the game at some point.

Off the Bench

Tell your players that the competition starts from the first day of practice, and though you are in charge, they will decide who plays in the game and who sits on the bench.

When the athletes work to get off the bench, the rest of the team will accept challenges more easily, and the coach will have no doubts about putting in one player for another. When a girl works hard to get on the court, she will work even harder to stay on the court because she won't want to lose her spot.

> **Controlled competition within the team creates a competitive spirit among the players.**

It always brings me joy to see the team's chemistry remain the same when a player comes off the bench and joins the game. This, however, rarely happens, as the players on the bench often cause the team to lose points before they actually get into the rhythm of the game. That is the coach's dilemma. Do you put them in the game anyway or leave them on the bench all the time? There will be a right time and you need to find it. Watch the girl on the bench in practice for something she does well, and when you see an opportunity for that play or skill, put her in the game. Maybe the team you are playing is not as good. Maybe you're ahead 12-3. Maybe you're behind 3-12. Or maybe she has a special serve that can change the flow of the game. You can also use her as a decoy or as a delay in the game, but remember to compliment her effort afterward.

In the Game

Time-outs are very valuable assets that coaches have during a game. Each team gets two per game, and coaches should carefully consider when to use them. Some coaches take a time-out to break a server, which I personally don't like. There are many ways to distract a server, and you can figure them out on your own. Coaches should save their time-outs for a more important reason.

Coaches can use a time-out to set up a play and to get a point, or even to win a close game. Never use your time-out to scream at your players. Instead, use it to tell them what is happening on the court, what the other team is doing right, and what your team can do better. Use the time to tell them what needs to be done in order to win the game, and save some time to encourage and motivate them. Point out the positives along with the negatives. Develop a look that says, "It's time to turn up the heat!" And say something funny before they go back on the court. That way, you put a smile on their faces and lift their spirits.

When the other team takes the time-out, use the time to encourage your players to continue playing hard. Tell them something they want to hear, such as the other team took the time-out to break your serve. Tell them that now is the time to show them what you are made of. Tell them to nail that serve. Tell them to show no mercy!

Keep it Positive

Unfortunately, many coaches dwell on the negatives and not the positives. For example, they will point to a player and say things such as, "You're killing us with your passing!" Try saying instead, "I know you can pass better than that. Now go out there and show them, because I know you can do it. I've seen it before." Or say, "Forget about the few bad passes. It's part of the game. Instead, think about the good ones you had before and try to recreate that." In this way, your players have positive information in their heads when they go back in the game.

> **Positive information in a timeout results in positive action in the time after.**

Substitutions

Substitutions are another valuable asset that coaches have to work with in a game. Like time-outs, there are a limited number of substitutions, so coaches should know how to use them and what they can achieve. I sometimes use a substitution in place of a time-out to get the break in the action that a time-out delivers. Or I will use a substitution to take a player out so I can speak to her, and then put her back in to deliver that information to the other players. Substitutions can also be used to get your specialist server or passer in the game. Sometimes a sub is used just to give your team a new look to which the other team must adjust.

You never want to make a sub if you have good flow to the game. Regardless of who is going in, the flow will always change somewhat, and most time it will change in the other team's favor. If you find that you have a good flow, wait until the flow breaks to make your substitution, especially if you just want to bring in other players. At the high school level, it is tough on a player to come into a tight game and give you a point.

If you have plans to use a special server to serve for the game point, make sure that player has had a chance to serve previously in the game. That way she will know the game's level of tension. At the higher level, you might see a coach bring in a server at game point to serve for the game, and even at that level the player might miss the serve because of the pressure.

Keep Your Cool

There will come an occasion when you get so angry at the ref for a bad call that you want to scream. But on the court, coaches speak to the ref through the captain. Coaches never shout across the court to the ref. If there continues to be a problem, first go to the second or down ref and calmly explain the situation to him or her. The down ref should then go across the court to the other ref if necessary, for further clarification. If you still don't like the explanation, back off and let the game continue. It's only a point. Win it back! If you continue in anger, you'll upset your team, embarrass yourself, and lose the respect of the parents and crowd.

If a ref is picking on a player, especially the setter, it is again the captain who approaches the ref. Call a time-out to explain the situation to your captain, and if she is calm and confident, have her go to the ref and say, "You're the only ref who calls her out on this. Can you consider that this is just the way her hands hit the ball," or something else appropriate to the situation. If the ref is picking on the setter and she is the captain, or if the captain is upset, take her out until she is calm enough to talk to the ref. If something intolerable continues to happen, keep a record of it and send a letter to the league's governing body.

Pre-Game Warm-Up with Drills

A pre-game warm-up starts at least 45 minutes before the game. Begin with five to seven laps around the volleyball court and then five minutes of stretching. Next you might go into some blocking drills and moving exercises across the net. Follow that with a drill for hitting, where you approach, jump, and swing, and then block and move across the net. Make sure the drill is done three times across the net, from the left side, middle and the right side.

You can take this drill even further. After you hit and block, turn and dive or sprawl to the floor, get up as quickly as possible, and repeat until it is done three times across the net. Stop and stretch again for five minutes and get some water.

Next, add some hitting to the drills where the setter sets a person who digs, and the digger then becomes the hitter. Do this back and forth a few times, and then rotate. This drill should be done at least 10 to 15 minutes before the referee blows the whistle to start the game. In this way, each team will have two- to five-minute periods to hit and serve. If your team hits first, take them off to the side and have them pass free balls, tips and digs afterward.

If you can, let your assistant coach supervise or conduct the drill. Use this time to watch the opposing team to determine which players are the big hitters and to figure out your game plan. If you are the only coach, have your team pass free balls to each other while you assess the other team. Never allow your team to watch the warm-up of the opposing team, because they might become intimidated by one or two hitters and a few good hits they saw. This can make them unnecessarily nervous at the start of the game.

After the Game

When the game is over, regardless of the result, the whole team must do a post-game cool-down which include some light jogging followed by light stretches. At this point you are trying to get the muscles to a normal stage, and pulling extra oxygen to the muscle will help prevent cramping or soreness. If players need to get ice, do it after the body cools down. If its temperature drops too quickly, the body can go into shock.

Keep your team together for a while and speak to them about the game as soon as possible, while it is still fresh in their minds. But don't keep them too long, especially if the team has lost the game. You can talk to them while they are stretching. If there is a serious incident that needs to be addressed, mention it and tell them you will deal with it at the next practice session. Use the next practice session to work on errors that were made during the game, and then go into a regular practice session later or the next day.

If you can follow these examples, you will have a team that loves you and will compete for you and everyone else they are representing.

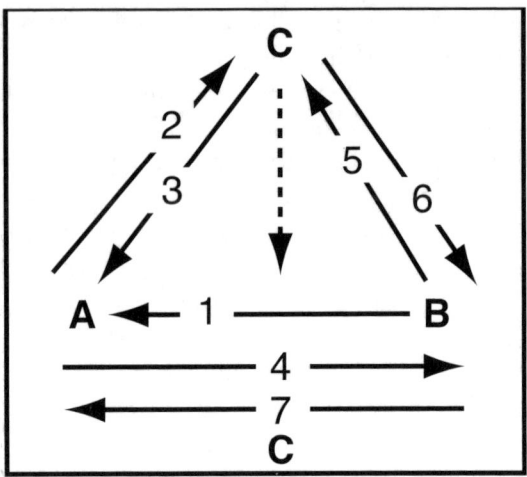

Passing Drill

Divide into groups of threes for this passing drill, using players A, B and C, with A on the left, B on the right and C in the middle. Each person will set and pass to the others in this order:
1. B tosses ball to A
2. A passes to C
3. C sets the ball back to A
4. A passes to B
5. B passes to C
6. C sets back to B
7. B passes to A

Here, C acts as the setter, even if she's not the setter, and A and B are the passers. The setter can stand on either side of the passers but should switch from A's left to A's right after 20 passes so that A and B can pass to their other side. After another 20 passes, C rotates to A, A moves to B and B becomes C and plays as the setter. Repeat the drill and then rotate again. Note: You can also hit and dig in this drill formation.

 # What Girls and Parents Should Know

I've coached and played on a men's national team (my current team, Big Apple Creole from New York City, won the men's AA division in 2004), and I've coached and played on a men's college team. I've coached women at the national, college, club and high school levels. Of all the teams I've coached, I've enjoyed coaching high school and club teams the most. In high school, girls are old enough to learn the proper techniques, smart enough to grasp the finer points, but have yet developed bad habits or routines from improper instruction.

For this book, I spoke to many of the girls I've coached and to their parents to find out what they learned and what they wished they had known before going off to college. Here you can benefit from their experiences.

Be Realistic

If you want to play in college, be realistic about your level of skills. If you really think you've got what it takes to play for Penn State or Stanford, go for it. You'll need to start working overtime in your sophomore and junior years, with lots of extra training and conditioning. Playing for a Division I team is truly exciting, but it comes with much added pressure. Look at Division II and Division III schools as an option, as each has a different balance between school work, college life and volleyball. One of my girls said this:

"I heard the varsity coach tell some freshman recruits that their job was to bring CDs for warm-up. I wanted to play, not sit on the bench, so I chose to play club rather than

Division I ball. We have a lot of fun and play great schools. I recommend this route."

Don't Pick a College Because of its Coach

Coaches move around, and by the time you actually hit the court on the first day, the coach who interviewed or recruited you may be long gone. It's sad but true. Also, your coach may leave the school during the time you are there, so keep this in mind when making your decision on which college to attend. One of my girls was recruited by a big name school. She met the coach in her senior year of high school, kept in touch over the summer, showed up for preseason, and one week later, the coach was fired. She told me how she felt about it:

"I was disappointed at first, but it worked out okay. I went for the game, not the coach. And the new coach is great too."

The best way to get a feel for the volleyball program at any particular school is to go to their games and meet the players. Tell them you're thinking of applying to that school, and see if you get a good feeling about them and the team. Many schools will arrange for you to spend some time with the team, perhaps over a weekend, so you can watch a game and practice and see the social life of the campus as well.

Investigate the College's Program for Volleyball and Academics

If you visit a school, meet the coach and learn that he or she is actually the lacrosse coach in the spring who is only filling in for volleyball, you may want to find out if the school is actively looking for a new volleyball coach.

When you visit a school and meet a coach, ask how the team prepares for games and what the team does afterward. Check the statistics on the Internet at a website such as www.ncaa.org or the school's own website. Find out how many games the team won last year and the previous year. If you can, find out how much money is allotted to the volleyball program in relation to the other sports programs at the school. Then compare it to other schools you're considering. You may find at one school the team travels to tournaments in cars while another school hires an air-conditioned luxury bus. Look at the schedule from last year to get a sense of where you'll be playing and how often. This is something you might want to discuss with your parents if you are going away to school and they intend to come to your games. Here's how one girl's team prepares for games.

"At my college, there's a lot of preparation for each game. On game day, we watch a tape of us or the other team playing, eat a certain number of hours before the game, watch more tape, do certain tasks and then get into the pre-game routine. No matter who we're playing, the prep is always the same."

Of course, you should check out the school's academic programs as well. Being an elite volleyball player, you will want a school that challenges your mind as well as your body. Make sure the school offers the courses you want to take and the major you might want to pursue, even if you are not certain what that is when you're applying to college.

Starting Off

All of my girls report that going off to college and playing volleyball gave them an instant community of teammates, mentors and friends. From the day they arrived on campus, they had 14 or so immediate friends who showed them around and advised them about school, classes and a new town, in a way that only teammates can. Playing on the volleyball team also made their names known on campus, much like it did in high school, but at a more respected level. Here's what some girls had to say:

"Nothing compares to coming to college for the first time and playing a fall sport. Football has only one game per weekend. Volleyball has a huge number of games. We play on Saturday, have Sunday off, and we're back on Monday for another game. And our names were all over the campus and in the school newspaper."

"I knew going from high school to college would be somewhat of a difficult transition, but I didn't realize when you're playing a sport, you automatically become a role model for younger kids. We do a lot of clinics and camps at our school and for me, it's not just about volleyball, it's about becoming an instant celebrity and representing your school and team at all times."

"Playing volleyball in college can be very overwhelming, but it's also so much fun."

Making the Commitment

Most of my girls reported that playing volleyball in college was a bigger, more serious commitment than high school, and that it was more intense. While missing practice because you had a big exam was acceptable in high school, it usually isn't in college. Because games are farther away, travel time increases. Many schools have games during the week and the team often takes off for a tournament on the weekends, traveling hundreds of miles by car and thousands by plane.

It's a common misconception that the commitment to a Division III team is less than it is to a Division II or Division I team. In fact, the time commitment is about the same. The difference is in the budgets for the teams, the recruiting methods, the length of the season and the scholarships offered.

Practice everywhere usually runs three hours a day, and most teams require that you lift weights in addition to practice.

"In season, we lift three times a week for one to one-and-a-half hours right after practice. We practice every day from 3:30 to 5:30, then lift weights and then eat."

"Our team lifts weights from 7:00 to 8:30 a.m. twice a week and we practice from 4:00 to 6:00 p.m. Then we all eat together."

With two to three hours of practice and an hour or so of weight training, managing your time becomes even more important. Most girls told me that they made it a point to keep up with their school work. One admitted to being more stressed out about school in the second semester than the first, because she didn't have volleyball in the second semester to help her manage her time and get her work done.

One of my girls went off to an Ivy League college and thought she wouldn't make the team as a "walk-on." In addition, she didn't want to make the commitment to a Division I team. Instead, she went out for the club team, and found it filled with Division I players who didn't want the commitment either. As a club team, they practiced two nights a week for two hours and played in a league with other club teams from nearby Division I schools. She played club ball all four years and loved her experience.

Another said that her own commitment to volleyball grew. She made a commitment to get stronger by lifting weights and conditioning. Another found that the competition was more intense.

"Coming in as a freshman, I had to fight for a spot on the team, even though I was drafted before my senior year in high school started. In college, I was constantly competing. Before we had even played another team, I had to prove I was good every day and with every play. It's all

about performance. Someone is always trying to take your spot. Also, I was playing against girls of my size and athleticism so I had to find a way to win in every situation. You do that by being aggressive and smart about each play."

Take the time to think about what you really want out of college volleyball before you get into it. This way, you can expect the unexpected and plan accordingly.

Each School is Different

Just as you will make a choice between a big school and a small school, and a school in a big city or a small town, every volleyball team will have a different goal or focus. Some college teams will spend a lot of time on technique and skills, and some will assume you know what you're doing by the time you get there. One girl reported that her technique improved a lot in college and another felt frustrated that she wasn't improving, as not much time was spent on it.

Many girls report that college is more specialized, with more rotations and substitutions, and that it's not about being a well-rounded player. You're likely to get more playing time if you excel in one area, like serving or blocking. Others say they work a lot on transition, and everyone should be prepared to play every position and to play it well.

One of my girls told me that college ball is always about the hit, and at her school they never did any passing drills. I might add here that she was one of the best passers I've ever coached. Another told me that her school had weak passers so they spent a lot of time on passing drills. You will find these situations in Division II and III colleges, and at these schools, the coaches will probably spend time on skills and technique before going to more complicated drills.

Some Differences

By the time you get to college, the level of coaching should be higher than in high school. Unfortunately in high school and club ball, many coaches are volunteers or are paid very little. In general, you can expect college coaches to have more experience in managing a team. You'll also find a larger playbook than you knew in high school or club. You'll learn that there's much more to the game than just scoring points.

College ball is faster. Passing and setting are two beats quicker. Passes go more directly to the setter and the sets are closer to the net. There's more emphasis on offensive action. Blocking is more important. Some teams emphasize defense, others don't. Teams and players are most likely to be at the same level. Games last longer and there is more competition. You will need to learn what is expected of you and then deliver it if you want to see more than the bench.

"In college certain parts of the game are about speed and strength, but a lot is how smart you play. My coach wasn't impressed with how hard I can hit the ball or how high I can jump. He was interested in the decisions I made on the court. It's all about court sense."

"In college, you have to fit with the system. When I came to preseason, I felt like I was behind because there was a system for hitting, a system for blocking, and I had to learn all that. Every person on the court has to work together."

"No matter what club team you have come from, if you work hard and play hard for every point, coaches see that and that's what they look for – girls who really go after every point and make good decisions on the court."

Advice

I went to see one of my girls play a college game and overheard one of the parents talking about her. He said, "That girl is small, but when she goes to hit, she looks like one of the big girls. Her form is perfect!" That particular girl had this advice to offer:

"Find college games on television, tape them and watch them. These players are some of the best in the country and just by watching them hit, serve, pass and set, you'll learn a lot. I used to love curling up in bed, crawling under the covers, turning out the lights and watching a college game on television. I think that's one of the reasons why my technique is as good as it is."

"Try to find a really good club team so that you can get a lot of exposure, because college coaches do most of their recruiting at qualifiers. As a senior in high school, I traveled 100 miles to find the right team."

"Girls need to realize that you can't depend only on high school or club team. You need to train outside, stay in shape, get stronger, improve your technique and develop your game. My advice is to take matters into your own hands and find the coaching you need to develop your skills."

Coping for Parents

I tell my girls to go easy on their parents when they go off to college. Most of the girls have parents who drove them back and forth to practice, who attended every game, often with cookies, and who spent their own money to stay in hotels during tournaments. After three or four years, the girls go off to college and leave their parents with a big void in their lives especially that first season when they are away for the first time. One parent had this to say:

"I really didn't know what to do with myself on weekends after my daughter went to college. I spent the fall driving hours to watch her play, and when the winter came, when I usually drove hours to tournaments around the country, it really hit me."

Because many girls go to college in a different town, parents go to fewer games. So be kind to them. Keep them in the loop. Tell them they can still bring cookies even if the school provides food for the team. Invite them to every game possible. Arrange to videotape a few games or practices for them if they can't get to games. Tell them about the other members of the team, and call them after big games to report the scores. Volleyball has been a big part of their lives, too, and they will be thrilled to be a part of your college volleyball experience, even from a distance.

Final Words

I don't want to think about where I'd be without volleyball. The game has given me enormous amounts of pleasure and a fulfilling career. Chances are, if you play well, work hard and get lucky, you will have a successful career – in something other than volleyball. Without a professional league, volleyball probably won't earn you a full-time living, unless you are lucky enough to become a coach at the college level. But it will give you invaluable skills in teamwork, management and endurance. So keep playing, and after all is said and done, go out there and teach a young girl to play. Nothing brings more joy to me than seeing someone I taught to play perform and compete on the court, and it's a terrific feeling to give back some of what has been given to you.